D1079984

It's not because
I want to die

ENS

Debbie Purdy
It's not because I want to die

With Gill Paul

ROTHERHAM LIBRARY SERVICE	
B515487	
Bertrams	06/04/2010
AN	£7.99
BSU	920 PUR

harper
true

HarperTrue
HarperCollins*Publishers*
77–85 Fulham Palace Road,
Hammersmith, London W6 8JB

www.harpercollins.co.uk

First published by HarperTrue 2010

1

© Debbie Purdy 2010

Debbie Purdy asserts the moral right to
be identified as the author of this work

A CIP catalogue record of this book
is available from the British Library

ISBN 978-0-00-735798-7

Printed and bound in Great Britain by
Clays Ltd, St Ives plc

All rights reserved. No part of this publication may be
reproduced, stored in a retrieval system, or transmitted,
in any form or by any means, electronic, mechanical,
photocopying, recording or otherwise, without the prior
permission of the publishers.

Mixed Sources
Product group from well-managed
forests and other controlled sources
www.fsc.org   Cert no. SW-COC-001806
© 1996 Forest Stewardship Council

FSC is a non-profit international organisation established to promote the
responsible management of the world's forests. Products carrying the FSC
label are independently certified to assure consumers that they come
from forests that are managed to meet the social, economic and
ecological needs of present and future generations.

Find out more about HarperCollins and the environment at
www.harpercollins.co.uk/green

Contents

Preface

'Jump!' the instructor yelled.

I obeyed instinctively, then immediately regretted it. What the hell was I doing jumping out of a perfectly good aeroplane 3,000 feet in the air?

'One thousand and one.' Training kicked in and I adopted the spread-eagle position, face down. Why am I doing this? What was I thinking?

'One thousand and two,' I counted aloud, as we'd been taught, then squinted upwards. Was there any way back into the plane? Surely there had to be. I was still attached by a static line that would pull my chute open. Could I climb up it?

'One thousand and three.' The Doc Martens I was wearing were too wide and my feet were shaking, hitting each side so rapidly I thought they might come loose and fall off. I can't believe I'm doing this, I thought. This is so stupid.

Terror was making me alert to every tiny sensation and I could feel the blood pumping hard through my veins.

'One thousand and four. Check, shit, malfunction. If your parachute hasn't deployed by the time you've finished counting, you're in trouble and it's time to open your secondary chute. Just then, though, I felt a gentle lift and I was pulled upright as my main chute opened. The static line detached and I felt intense relief as I looked up at the billowing white canopy. I've never felt so grateful to see anything!

The relief was short-lived because I then looked down and saw that there was nothing between me and the ground. I was falling more slowly, but I was still very definitely falling.

It was deathly quiet up there, and very peaceful. I'd been told to scope out a big yellow cross on the ground and aim for that using the toggles on either side of my chute to change direction, but I couldn't even see the damn cross. Where the hell was it? I spotted a parachute in front of me and thought I would just aim for that in the hope that it was aiming for the cross. All the guys who were jumping with me that day had seemed cool, calm and confident, so I figured that whoever I was following was going the right way.

I played with the toggles but wasn't sure how much effect I was having. I kept aiming for the guy ahead and praying that he wasn't headed for a tree. I still couldn't see the cross, but by that stage I didn't care if I was miles away so long as I hit the ground with both feet and didn't end up hanging from an electricity cable or the upper branches of a tree.

Suddenly the ground was right there and I closed my eyes and went into autopilot, rolling on impact as we'd been taught. When I opened my eyes, I looked down my body to make sure nothing was broken or bleeding and realised my arm was lying on a yellow cross. I'd landed right on top of the target. The guy I had been following was a few hundred yards further on. There was no blood. I was alive and intact.

The instructor who filled out my logbook later wrote, 'GATW,' meaning 'Good all the way.' I didn't mention that it was a matter of luck rather than careful control. I felt fantastic. Sheer terror turned to sheer exhilaration and I asked, 'When can I have another go?'

That was in 1981 and I was 17 years old.

In 1995, fourteen years later, a doctor said to me, 'When I first saw you, I thought you had MS,' and inside my head I started to count, one thousand and one.

He organised an MRI scan and a lumbar puncture. One thousand and two.

It *was* MS and I was in freefall, scared and lonely. One thousand and three.

I walked into the arrivals hall at Singapore's Changi Airport and saw Omar waiting. I felt a gentle lift and I was upright again – still falling, but I knew I was safe and would be able to control my descent.

I haven't hit the ground yet. What follows is the story of my journey down so far.

It's not because
I want to die

Chapter 1

A Heart in Chains

In January 1995, at the age of 31, I had recently moved to Singapore and was earning my keep with a pen. (Well, a Mac laptop, but that's product placement!) I wrote brochure copy for an adventure travel company, and music reviews and features for a number of magazines. A welcome perk of my job was that I got into all the live music clubs free, so of course I was having fun (especially as the bars wouldn't take money from me for drinks). I shared a flat with an Australian bass player, Belinda, and a Japanese teacher, Tetsu, and was dating my fair share of men without having anyone serious on the scene.

One night Belinda came home from work raving about a band she had seen playing in a club called Fabrice's. 'There are seven gorgeous men,' she said, 'and they're explosive on stage. You have to see them.'

'What are they called?'

'The Cuban Boys.'

I rang *Music Monthly* to ask if they'd be interested in a review and they said, 'Sure.'

I was interested in exploring why foreign musicians were frequently paid so little. I had dreams of doing some investigative journalism to rival *All the President's Men*. It was a genuine problem, but I have to admit I was looking for a problem I could bury myself in solving.

I turned up at Fabrice's on the afternoon of 25 January, toting my notebook and camera, to sit in on the band's rehearsals. My first thought was that 'the Cuban Boys' was a strange name for a group that had seven blokes and three girls in it. My second thought was that Belinda had been exaggerating. Only two of the band members, Emilio and Juan Carlos, were particularly good-looking, while the rest could be described as having 'good personalities'.

It was the band leader, Omar Puente, who came over to talk to me for the interview, and I thought he seemed a bit Mafioso with his little moustache. He sat opposite me looking very serious and frowning in concentration as we struggled to overcome the language barrier. I spoke English, some Norwegian and a little French, while Omar spoke Spanish, Russian and a little French, so French it was. It took me about twenty minutes to get a single quotable sentence. (I wasn't 100 per cent sure of how much I understood, but he didn't read English, so I was unlikely to be sued.)

I picked up the camera and motioned that I wanted to take a picture of them playing. Omar indicated in sign language that they should get changed into their performance outfits, instead of the casual clothes they were wearing.

'No, don't bother,' I said. 'If you could just play a number for me as you are, that would be fine.' I motioned towards the stage.

When they started playing, I was instantly impressed. They had a really good sound, and Omar's violin-playing was fantastic. The repertoire comprised modern and traditional Cuban dance music, but Omar also did a little Bach as a solo and I could hear humour as well as hard work and technique in his playing. On the violin he obviously felt in control; he was a complete master of it.

In the middle of the set, the band launched into a version of 'La Cucaracha'. The percussionist, Juan Carlos, stood on his chair and put one leg on his conga drum. Then they all stopped playing and did pelvic thrusts in time to the 'Da-da-da-da dah-dah' bit in the chorus. It was crude and obscene, but mesmerising.

I came back to Fabrice's later that night to watch the proper show. The band was not dressed up in their performance shirts, so I figured Omar had been trying to be interesting for the press. (Now I realise it was *me* he was trying to impress.) He had a very charismatic presence, interacting with the audience and chatting to them between numbers, and moving around the stage with ease. He wasn't the best-looking band member, but you couldn't take your eyes off him, mainly because you wanted to see what he would do next. All the band members moved with an easy, natural rhythm, the music was note-perfect, and their set was a huge hit with the regulars at Fabrice's.

After they finished playing, Omar walked off stage and came over to sit beside me, bringing his friend Rolando, who spoke a bit of English and tried to translate for us.

'Will you be nice about us in your magazine?' Omar and Rolando asked. Well, that's what they were trying to ask.

'Of course,' I said. They were so earnest and incredibly entertaining to watch that being anything less than glowing about them would have been like kicking a puppy.

The two of them would feverishly converse in Spanish, words tripping over one another, for several minutes before Omar would try to say something in English.

'Do you live in Singapore?' he asked next, and I told him that I did.

Our scintillating conversation floundered a bit when one of Rolando's girlfriends arrived, but Omar didn't leave my side for the rest of the evening except to get back on stage and play the second set.

At two or three in the morning, when Singapore was winding down, I was in the habit of stopping at a market for an early breakfast on the way home. I invited Omar to join me so we could continue trying to talk. We borrowed an English–Spanish dictionary, as Rolando didn't consider his role much fun and the girlfriend clearly was. We walked down to the market and bought bowls of congee (a kind of rice porridge) and some other snacks, and sat at a roadside table to eat.

Now we were away from his job and the band, Omar dropped his earlier, more fatherly persona and started to be flirtatious, touching my arm and offering me bites of his food to sample. It dawned on me that he thought I had asked him on a date. I was just being professional and finishing the interview (I think). He was all smiles and charm until he accidentally bit on a piece of chilli, which ruined his composure. His eyes started watering and he was coughing and spluttering. I handed him a bottle of water to cool his mouth down. Not the most romantic start, and nothing to indicate that this would be the love of my life.

I still hadn't asked about how much the band was being paid, so I opened the dictionary at the word 'fee'. Omar signalled, 'Twenty,' with his fingers.

'A day?' I was horrified.

He nodded.

I thought we were talking about Singapore dollars, which are worth a lot less than US dollars. Believing that the band was being paid a tiny fraction of what their Singaporean counterparts would earn, my trade-unionist instincts kicked in and my hackles rose. After some frantic investigation, though, I realised that he was telling me how much their daily allowance was, rather than their total fee, and he was talking in US dollars.

I later learned that their income had also been affected by a bad business decision. Most musicians pay an agent fee to whoever got them the job. For this type of long-term contract, it's usually no more than 15 per cent, and if two or more agents are involved they share the fee. Omar had been a band leader for a short time and his business skills were only marginally better than his language ones. Consequently, his limited (to put it politely) English meant that the Cuban Boys were paying two agents 15 per cent each, which resulted in the ten Cubans receiving just 70 per cent of the fee. It didn't seem right, but no one person was to blame. The band saved most of their pay to buy instruments, as they would need better equipment to be the next 'super group'. I could see they would also need better business sense.

We had been speaking at cross-purposes and not even in the same language. It's hard to make sense when you have to flick through a whole dictionary to locate every word, and even when you find the right one, cultural references mean you still speak at cross-purposes.

After I'd finished eating, I stood up to leave, laying my hands against my cheek to indicate that I needed to sleep. Dawn was breaking and people with normal jobs were starting to make their way to work. Omar asked, 'Fabrice's?' and I realised he was inviting me to come to the gig that evening. I couldn't make it, so I shook my head and said, '*Au revoir. A bientôt.*' The Singapore music scene was tiny and I had no doubt we would bump into each other again before too long.

Years later we would still disagree on the details of the day we met. I remember wearing a little black dress, looking sexy and sophisticated, whereas he said I was wearing a white T-shirt and a black skirt. (I know he's wrong because he says I wasn't wearing a bra!) I probably had the skirt and T-shirt on in the afternoon for the interview (but with a bra) and the dress on in the evening when I returned to the club for the set. He says it was me who came on to him, whereas I know it was definitely him. He says he was initially attracted by my bottom, and even said so in an *Observer* article in 1998. (Talking about the size of a girl's bottom in print must be grounds for divorce!) I wasn't really that interested in him at first, but I loved the way he played violin. We had the same experience, but we both have different memories of it. Mine, of course, are right!

A couple of days after meeting Omar, Belinda and I went to a jam session at Harry's Bar – all the musicians in Singapore ended up there on Sundays because if you played you got free drinks – and as soon as we walked in I spotted Omar. He came straight over, but there was an awkward silence because there wasn't much we could say without someone to translate for us. Normally, you would move on and talk to someone else at this point, but Omar sat down. We listened to the music and had a few drinks. Every time a male friend of mine came over to chat, Omar positioned himself between me and the other man like a bodyguard and watched intently. I wasn't sure that I wanted this sort of attention, but I felt flattered to be pursued by someone so 'present'. Gradually I realised that he seemed to have decided I was his.

Back at the flat I shared with Tetsu and Belinda, Belinda quizzed me about him. 'He looks pretty interested. How about you?'

'A moot point – we can't even discuss the weather. He seems nice, but he could be an axe murderer for all I know.'

Belinda couldn't communicate with him either, and his easy charm and macho display at Harry's rang warning bells. Besides, her own experience of Latin musicians hardly endeared Omar to her. She herself knew charming Latin men who would quickly make beautiful declarations of love, mean it when they said it, but then leave the room and fall in love with someone else, before finally going home to a wife and kids.

Omar was only a year and a bit older than me – 33 when we met – but he took responsibility for the whole band, and being a band leader is probably the closest thing to being a parent you can get without having to change nappies. Omar could never relax properly at Fabrice's, where he had nine Cuban kids to look out for. The language barrier was the main problem for them all, but there was always something ready to trip them up. They had a safe refuge on stage. When the band members were together, they could be themselves – crazy and funny, a little wild but always in control – and they had their fearless leader, who was, like any parent, ready to do anything to protect them. Omar loved his band, his music and his life. There was no language barrier with a violin in Omar's hands.

He may have been the responsible one, the father figure of the Cuban Boys, but it didn't stop him messing around on stage. One night not long after I'd met Omar, he introduced the band – 'Juan Carlos on conga, Julio on drum kit …' – and then he pointed to me in the audience, making everyone turn to look, and said, *'Allí tienes a la mujer que tiene mi corazón encadenado.'*

'What did he just say?' I pestered a friend, who was laughing by my side.

He translated: 'There's the woman who has my heart in chains.'

I went crimson (something I was to do a lot with Omar). I liked the fact that he was so public about trying to win me over. It was flattering ... but still I had my reservations. Latin men and all that.

It's difficult forming an impression of someone at the best of times, even more so when you don't speak the same language and you can't have a conversation, but while watching Omar perform I felt I was getting to know the man. Of all instruments, I think the violin is closest to a voice and I believe you can get a sense of who a person is by the way that they play. Omar's character came across in his music, and what I saw was someone who was witty and intelligent and caring. It would have taken me years to work that out based on our staccato verbal communications, but his violin-playing told me who he was.

For two and a half weeks I saw Omar nearly every night at Fabrice's or, earlier in the evening, at one of Singapore's other music venues (of which there were many). As soon as I arrived, he would stride across the room to kiss me hello and stand by my side, warning off competitors. He'd play his set on stage, then walk straight over the raised area that adjoined the stage to come back and stand by me. He seemed devoted, but still all my friends were saying, 'Latin musicians? You don't want to go near one.'

On Valentine's Day I went for dinner with another man, an engineer who was a friend of the manager of Fabrice's. We'd

9

known each other for a couple of months and he was very attractive, so when he'd asked me out I'd thought, Great.

He was charming and attentive, and we had a lively conversation over our meal. Then, at midnight, we drifted along to Fabrice's, because that's where everyone went in the early hours. As soon as we walked in, though, I spotted Omar and felt uncomfortable. I didn't want him to see me with another man. He got up on stage to play his set and I led my date over to join a group of friends, making sure I sat at the opposite side of the table from him.

My date was puzzled by my hot–cold attitude and asked, 'Do you want to dance, Debbie?'

'No, not really. I'm fine, thanks.' I realised I didn't want Omar to see me on a date. I had been proclaiming disinterest for a couple of weeks, but my reluctance to let him see me with another man spoke volumes and I had to admit, to myself at least, that this charming enigma was burrowing his way under my skin.

My date came over to sit beside me and slipped his arm around my shoulders. Immediately I jumped up. 'Must go and chat to someone,' I gabbled. 'I'll be back in a minute.'

The poor man didn't know what was going on. Every time he tried to lay a finger on me, I'd quickly check whether we were in Omar's line of sight from the stage, and if we were I'd jump up manically and find someone else to talk to. I made sure we weren't alone, inviting everyone I knew to join us at our table. By the end of the evening my poor date had certainly got the message that I wasn't interested in him romantically – either that or he had concluded that I was deeply neurotic.

I didn't talk to Omar that night because he was working and we'd left by the time he came off stage, but several times I saw him watching me with a confused expression. For my part, that was the night I finally accepted that I was hugely attracted to him. Latin musician or not, I was going to have to go out with this man. It didn't look as though I had a choice.

The next day when I got home from work at the adventure travel company, Belinda said to me, 'You'll never guess what! *He* called. Several times.'

'Omar? He called here? What did he say?' Belinda didn't speak any Spanish either, so I knew it couldn't have been a long chat.

'He said, "Party. Tonight," and he left the address. That was all.'

A mutual friend of ours was having a party that evening and Omar had phoned to make sure I would be there. I think I blushed I was so pleased. 'What do you reckon?'

'Oh, Debbie, for goodness' sake, just go for it and save us all the hassle. Please.'

I grinned. That's exactly what I planned to do.

The party was at the home of an American guy and he'd set up a barbecue on his balcony. It was late when I got there and the main room was heaving with people. I stood in the entrance, peering around to see who I knew, and locked eyes with someone staring straight back at me: Omar. He hurried over.

'You came,' he said in English. 'That's good.'

He got me a drink and Rolando came over to translate for a while so we could have a slightly more sophisticated conversation than our usual monosyllables. When Omar went to the barbecue to get some food, I took the opportunity to ask Rolando a question that had been on my mind: was Omar married? I pointed at Rolando's wedding finger and motioned a ring. He shook his head, but I wanted to double-check, given my distrust of Latinos, musicians and men in general, so I asked Rolando directly.

He frowned and scratched his cheek before saying, 'I'm not sure. He's never mentioned anything about a wife. We just play together. We aren't close. Sorry – I can't help you there.'

I later found out that Omar and Rolando had been best friends for fifteen years and knew all there was to know about each other. Rolando hadn't wanted to answer my question in case he contradicted something that Omar had told me, so he'd just avoided it. It was the same for all the band members: they would have laid down their lives for each other. They were a long way from home, and they depended on each other, so economy with the truth over romantic interludes was second nature. It was behaviour like this that gave Latin musicians their reputation (but they also have a reputation for steadfast loyalty, and that's true as well).

I circulated, chatting to people I knew, while Omar hovered by my side doing his bodyguard impression. As the party broke up, we went back to Harry's Bar and I knew that I was happy with Omar beside me. Everyone was watching us and wondering, Will they? Won't they? because his pursuit of me was good gossip in our orbit.

In the early hours of the morning he walked me home to my flat and I was amused because he did that gentlemanly thing of constantly moving so that he was between me and the road. I tried to explain to him that the tradition derived from days when ladies didn't want their beautiful gowns to get splashed by passing carriages, which was hardly likely to be a problem in modern-day Singapore. First of all, I had left my beautiful gown at home, and secondly, the roads were bone-dry. I'm not sure he understood my explanation, delivered in a mixture of French, English and sign language, like an elaborate game of charades.

Shortly after that he kissed me for the first time, which was nice. More than nice. He remained a perfect gentleman, though, dropping me back at the flat I shared with Belinda and Tetsu, and asking if he could see me the next evening. He gave me his phone number and taught me how to greet the person who answered the phone: '*Quiero hablar con mi mulato lindo.*' I repeated the phrase until I could say it to his satisfaction, and we kissed one last time before he headed off down the road, turning to give me a wave as he left my sight.

He and the band members loved it when I phoned the next day – I thought I was greeting them and commenting on the wonderful day; in fact I was asking to speak to 'my beautiful mulatto'!

Nevertheless, the next night I was right there when Omar played his set at Fabrice's and he gazed straight at me as he sang many of the numbers. When he was introducing the band, he went through all their names, then at the end said, '*Allí tienes a la mujer que tiene mi corazón encadenado,*' and I knew without being told what that meant. I had his heart in chains. From then on he said it every night I was there.

The evening after we'd slept together for the first time, he walked off stage in the middle of the Cuban Boys' set and came over to kiss me, which was incredibly romantic. Our friends in the audience cheered and clapped. I blushed, because I embarrass easily, but I loved it at the same time.

Neither of us had much money, but it didn't matter – we were living in a beautiful city, had some great friends, and both of us had jobs that we loved and would have *paid* for the privilege of doing. We had the added advantage of being welcome guests at most of the places we wanted to go. (It seems silly, but business is business and I was more welcome than Omar because I could publicise the venue.) We would talk in odd words and phrases we'd picked up of each other's language, supplemented by whole sentences when Rolando or someone else was around to translate for us. After the Cuban Boys' set at Fabrice's, we would go for breakfast at the market or pick up some food from the 7-Eleven in Orchard Road, then walk home together in the early morning light. It was lovely, despite the fact that I sometimes had to go straight to work without any sleep.

I had a book of Chinese horoscopes in my room and Omar asked me when my birthday was, then worked out that I was born in the Year of the Rabbit, so from then on he called me

'Rabbit'. That was his pet name for me. He was born in the Year of the Ox, so I didn't do the same.

We had a fantastic two weeks together, full of music and city lights (and I guess the food and wine didn't hurt the atmosphere). At the beginning of March a neurology appointment I had booked in Brighton meant I had to go to England. Omar and the band were going to Indonesia for a month to do some gigs at a club in Jakarta.

As we parted on that night in early March, he said to me, 'See you in a month, Rabbit.'

My life was perfect. I was doing things I loved in a new and exciting city, and I'd just met someone who made the sunniest day a little brighter. I was living a dream, but I didn't really realise how lucky I was. I took it all for granted. I guess I felt entitled to everything life could offer. As I boarded the plane, I couldn't wait to get back and carry on living my wonderful life.

Chapter 2

Wading through Honey

The reason I had a neurology appointment was because I'd been noticing my body behaving a bit strangely over the last year or so. There were lots of little things – nothing major – but they seemed to indicate something odd was going on.

The weirdest incident had been in August 1994, when I'd collapsed in the street back in Yorkshire, where I lived at the time. I'd spent the day walking around Leeds city centre with an American friend called Greg, who was thinking of moving to the UK and wanted to explore what kind of work he might be able to get. We'd walked for miles into recruitment companies and coffee shops. Greg needed to get a feel for the city as well as the jobs. On the way back, when we were only a couple of hundred yards from my home in Bradford, all of a sudden my legs gave way beneath me and I collapsed on the pavement.

'What's going on? Did you trip?' Greg stretched out an arm to help me.

'I don't know.' I grabbed his hand and tried to pull myself up, but my legs wouldn't take my weight: they were weak and unresponsive. 'Isn't that strange?' I felt silly more than anything else. Greg was super-fit, and although I knew I'd been getting a bit out of condition, I hadn't thought it was quite that bad.

'Can't you get up?'

'I just need to rest a while and then I'll be fine.' At least, I hoped I would.

'Try again,' Greg coaxed me, concerned and more than a little embarrassed to be seen with a woman who was sitting in the gutter on a busy main road. People passing clearly thought I was drunk.

I summoned all my strength, clung on to Greg's arm and tried to haul myself up, but my legs still wouldn't support my weight. An image of the Billy Connolly sketch in which he imitates a Glaswegian 'rubber drunk' flashed through my head. I had rubber legs, it seemed, without a drop of booze having passed my lips.

'It's no use,' I said. 'We'll have to call a cab.'

Greg seemed glad to be given something to do. Before long he was helping me into the back of a local cab. Two minutes later Greg and the driver got me into the house by holding me on either side and more or less carrying me until I was ensconced in an armchair in my front room.

'You have to see a doctor,' Greg insisted. 'That shouldn't happen. Shall I phone for someone?'

'If you want to do something useful,' I told him, 'make a cup of tea.' A universal British cure-all.

We sat and drank our tea and talked about the job opportunities Greg had found, and a few hours later my legs seemed to be back to normal, so I brushed aside all his nagging about doctors and tests and making a fuss. I'm an arrogant sod and prided myself on my physical prowess. I'd completed several parachute jumps, skied, played netball for my county team and learned to waterski off Hong Kong, so a day's walking shouldn't have fazed me.

Over the next couple of weeks, though, I gave it some more thought, wondering what was going on and whether I needed to do anything about it. I'd noticed a few other odd things. For example, I was a keen horse-rider, but now it took me quite a lot of effort to get my foot in the stirrup and swing myself up on to the horse. I'd always had a good seat, which you achieve by using your thigh muscles to hold your position on the saddle, but recently I'd been a bit like a sack of potatoes being bounced around as the horse cantered across the field.

Then there was my eyesight. I'd noticed that words were getting slightly blurred on the page. Curiously, it seemed to get worse when I was too hot. I figured that everyone's eyesight deteriorates as they get older, but I was only 31. Should it be starting that early?

Having lived all over the world, I'd been back in the UK for almost four years before I moved to Singapore in September 1994 and I blamed the British climate for many of my symptoms. I'd put on a bit of weight, so that could have been one factor, but I mostly blamed the sedentary indoor life I'd been leading. When I was out in the Far East, I was always rushing around waterskiing, swimming or cycling. On Christmas Day we would spit-roast a turkey on the beach, decorate palms with tinsel and splash around in the surf. Back in cold, rainy Bradford, Christmas meant eating far too much, drinking more than was good for you and falling asleep in front of the TV.

I had come back to the UK in 1990 to help look after my mum. She had been ill for several years and my sisters had been shouldering the responsibility. I felt it was time that I shared it. When Mum died in 1992, it came as an incredible shock, despite the fact that we'd all known she was ill. It was nice to get close to my family again and I'd planned on staying for a bit, but I was beginning to feel old, putting on weight and generally feeling 'not right'.

Then, in 1994, a friend of mine, a singer called Mildred Jones, called to invite me out to Singapore, where she had a contract at the piano bar in the Hilton Hotel. She said I could stay with her and she would introduce me to people who would help me to find work.

It was an irresistible offer and I took less than a nanosecond to reply. 'Sure. I'm on my way.'

I found people to look after the house I owned in Bradford and booked a plane ticket for 24 September. Before I left, I decided to pay a quick visit to my GP just to be on the safe side.

I sat down in his surgery and let the words pour out. 'I've been a bit out of sorts recently. I'm sure it's partly grieving for Mum, but also I've put on some weight that I need to lose, and living in the UK doesn't really suit me. I prefer a hot climate and an outdoor lifestyle. Anyway, I'm solving it by moving out to Singapore next week. What do you think?'

'That all sounds very sensible,' the doctor said, a bit bowled over by the speed at which I can talk when I get going.

All the symptoms I presented him with were subjective: a bit tired, feeling slightly weak, generally depressed. I answered my own questions as I spoke and he just agreed with me. I didn't have a massive tumour anywhere. I wasn't in pain. There was nothing concrete that might have made him suspicious that there was anything going on. Besides, I didn't want to hear any bad news. All I wanted was reassurance. I had a plane to catch and an exciting new life waiting for me, so I more or less presented him with a *fait accompli*.

'So I'm fine to go?'

'Yes,' he said, looking somewhat baffled by the onslaught. 'Have a good time.'

The symptoms didn't go away in Singapore's sunnier climes, though. If anything, they got worse. I started walking everywhere to try and get fit but found my legs were tired after short distances, and I couldn't swim as many lengths of a swimming pool as I used to. Then, within three weeks of my arrival, I got a phone call that shattered my world. It was from my auntie Judy's husband, Uncle Paul.

'Debbie?' he said. 'Your dad is dead.'

'What? You're joking!' He'd come out with it so abruptly that I assumed it was a sick practical joke, even though I knew Paul would never be so cruel.

Auntie Judy took the phone from him. 'I'm so sorry,' she said. 'I'm afraid he had a heart attack.'

'Really? My dad? Are you sure?' He was such a life-force it didn't seem possible.

'His girlfriend was with him at the time, but there was nothing that could be done. He was dead before the ambulance got here.' She was trying hard to hold back the tears and not doing too well.

I had talked to Dad the week before I left the UK. He'd been living in the States and was due to arrive in England a couple of days before I left so that we would see each other, but work had delayed him. I'd enquired about changing my flight, but it was a cheap ticket and to change it would cost almost as much as I'd paid for it in the first place. Instead we'd agreed to meet when he came to Southeast Asia a few months later.

I put the phone down and looked around at the friends in the room. They were watching me with concern, having picked up the gist of the call.

'I'm an orphan,' I told them, before bursting into tears.

The shock was monumental. How could there have been no warning signs at all? It felt like the end of the world.

One of Mildred's friends bought me a plane ticket home for the funeral, and my sisters, Tina, Gillian and Carolyn, and my brother, Stephen, and I clung to each other in disbelief. More than two years had passed since Mum's funeral, but it felt very recent. We hadn't lived with Dad for a long time, but we still felt bereft. Even in your 30s you want to feel that you have someone to fall back on. Uncle Tony and Auntie Judy, his brother and sister, were inconsolable. They had been close to him all their lives and the three of them adored each other.

A few days after the funeral I caught a flight back to Singapore. I didn't know what to do, but I wanted to stay busy or I would have sat and sobbed all day long. I'd moved into the flat with Belinda and Tetsu, and there were always people milling around and gigs to attend. I said yes to every invitation as a way of keeping myself afloat, otherwise I would have sunk under the weight of grief.

Two weeks after I got back, in November 1994, Auntie Judy called again, utterly heartbroken. She was stuttering and could hardly get the words out. 'Tony died. It was a heart attack.' Apparently he was making a cup of tea when he collapsed and was dead before he hit the floor. He didn't even disturb anything in the kitchen.

I felt numb this time. It was all too much. I didn't have the money to fly home for another funeral, so I grieved in Singapore. Still shell-shocked about Dad, it was hard to take in this new piece of information.

Then there was a third blow. On the night of Uncle Tony's funeral, Auntie Judy died as well. I think she died of a broken heart, because she was so distraught at losing her brothers. They'd all three been so close in life that somehow it made sense that they died close together. I think it would have been unbearable for the ones left behind if it had been any other way. Nevertheless, it was devastating for the family to have three funerals in a row.

I put my head down and tried to get on with life in Singapore. What else could I do? Being on the other side of the world helped to make it seem unreal. Part of me still felt that when I next went home they'd all be there, same as ever.

Mildred was like a mother to me in this period, sweeping me up into her vast group of friends and making sure I didn't mope around too much. Belinda saw to it that I ate and slept, and I still had my work for the adventure travel brochures and the music magazines. I spent most evenings at clubs and live music venues, and I'd usually be up on the dance floor.

I love dancing, and I was lucky enough to have been born with a decent sense of rhythm (tone deaf, but I could move), but strangely I found my body wasn't moving the way I wanted it to. I felt as though I was wading through honey, or as if I was wearing trainers and they were sticking to chewing gum that someone had dropped on the floor. (Unlikely, as the Singaporean government had banned the sale of gum.) It wasn't that I was tired; my movements just felt slow and strange. I thought it was because of the extra weight I'd put on back in England, so I borrowed a bike to cycle around town and get fitter. I wasn't fat, but I definitely wasn't as toned as I'd have liked to be.

Soon after Dad's funeral I began to have the weirdest headaches I'd ever had in my life. It felt as if something was reaching inside my skull and squeezing my brain. They only lasted for a few seconds at a time, but they were intensely painful. I became convinced that I must have a brain tumour. This was in the days before Mo Mowlam, the Labour Secretary of State for Northern Ireland, died as a result of her brain tumour, and my preconception was that they were quite a sexy thing to have. I'd go into hospital, have my head shaved, undergo brain surgery and then recuperate. Everything would be better within a few months and I thought it would be quite exciting. I could be 'heroic Debbie' with my bald head, admired for my stoicism.

I flew back to England to spend Christmas with my family, and while I was up in Yorkshire I went to see a GP, presented him with my self-diagnosis and asked to be referred for a CT scan. He didn't play along, though.

'Let me put it this way,' he said. 'We doctors have to do a kind of jigsaw puzzle. Say you find a bit of blue sky. You might not know exactly where it fits, but you know it's sky.'

I concentrated hard, trying to work out how this related to my headaches and muscle weakness.

'There's nothing physically wrong with you,' he continued. 'You were grieving for your mum and felt terrible about losing her, and then your dad died. It's all happened at once. I'm going to refer you to a therapist who can help you to talk it through.'

So that was it! Depression wasn't as sexy as a brain tumour, so I was a bit disappointed. I still clung to my 'heroic Debbie' image. I'd never been the depressive type and I wasn't sure I believed his diagnosis, but doctors are always right, aren't they?

I went down to stay with my uncle Paul in Brighton before my flight back to Singapore. As it happened, his friend's son had had a brain tumour and they urged me to get a second opinion. They just had an instinct that my doctor's diagnosis wasn't quite right.

I went to see my uncle's GP, a smart, no-nonsense woman with a surgery in Brighton. After listening to my description of the symptoms, she got me to lie down and drag my heel up my shin – first the left heel, then the right. I managed it, but there must have been something she didn't like about the way I did it. She ran a few more tests and asked me lots of questions, then said she was going to refer me to a neurologist.

Good, I thought. A neurologist sounded serious and important. Surely he would be able to send me for a brain scan and we'd be a little closer to coming up with a diagnosis, something unusual and interesting.

I was warned it would be a couple of months before the appointment came through, so I went back out to Singapore, still secretly convinced I had a brain tumour. I didn't tell Mildred or anyone else about my theory because it sounded melodramatic. In answer to their questions I said, 'Oh, there's nothing wrong with me,' imagining that when I finally told them the truth they would think, Poor thing, she was trying to be brave and play it down when all along she was suffering terribly.

Peter, my boss at the adventure travel company, seemed to be happy with my work because he asked if I would like to go on a scuba-diving course on Tioman Island, off the Malaysian coast. Would I ever! The idea was that I would write a diary of my experiences that would be published by *8 Days*, a magazine about what's on in Singapore. Peter, his partner and other colleagues could already dive and they wanted someone who could write about the learning experience. Once I could dive,

Peter promised that he would send me to review other scuba sites they covered.

I loved the resort on Tioman, a genuine paradise island with white sand and palm trees. The staff were bottle-feeding a little orphan monkey whose mother had been killed by poachers and everyone liked playing with him because he was so cute and cuddly.

I found the underwater world magical. If you learn to dive off the British coast, the visibility is likely to be measured in inches, feet if you're lucky, but in the South China Sea we could see way off. It was incredible to be underwater marvelling at the rainbow-coloured fish and strange tentacled creatures, and my worries about a brain tumour faded into the distance. How could I possibly be ill when I felt so alive and exhilarated?

Back in Singapore, reality intruded when I got word that my neurology appointment would be on 6 March and the therapy session a couple of weeks later. It was time to make another trip to the UK, just after I'd started going out with Omar.

'You won't send anyone else on the diving trips, will you?' I asked Peter. 'You'll definitely wait for me to come back?' I think I'd have cancelled the appointments otherwise.

'It will all be here waiting for you,' he promised. 'Good luck!'

On 6 March 1995 I turned up for my neurology appointment at the Royal Sussex County Hospital. I recited the list of symptoms, mentioned that my parents had died recently and ventured my humble opinion that I might have a brain tumour.

'Lie down on the bed,' the neurologist instructed. 'Tell me what you can feel.'

I could see he was holding a pin, and as far as I was concerned he just touched it lightly on my foot, pressing a bit harder as he moved up my leg, then stabbing it into my thigh. That's what I told him.

'Actually, I applied the same pressure all the way up,' he told me.

I blinked in surprise. It seemed I had reduced sensation in the lower parts of my legs. What on earth did that mean?

'I'm sending you for an MRI scan,' he said. 'We'll talk after that.'

I went back to my auntie Pat and uncle Dennis's house where I was staying, puzzled by the fragments of information I'd gleaned. Why would a brain tumour cause reduced sensation in my lower legs? Was that why I'd been feeling weird when I was dancing, and why I'd collapsed in the street that day with Greg?

I'd heard it took months for MRI appointments to come through, but mine only took about ten days. Why was it so fast? Was it due to mega-efficiency on the part of the hospital, just good luck, or had the neurologist told them it was urgent?

'It will take about forty-five minutes,' the radiographer told me. 'You have to lie very still on a bed that will slide inside a hollow tube, where we will take pictures of your insides a bit like a 3D X-ray. It's a bit noisy in there, so you'll need to wear some earplugs.'

I lay down on the bed, earplugs in place and a call button in my hand in case I got a sudden attack of claustrophobia. I was swept into the machine. There was a moment of silence, then a cacophony of clanking and long piercing beeps and a churning, whirring sound. After only a few minutes the noise stopped and I was sliding out again.

'What's up? You said it would take longer.'

'I've got all I need,' the radiographer told me.

'You've found something, haven't you? Is it a brain tumour?'

'The consultant will study the images and discuss the results with you. He has to interpret them.'

I knew they had found something. They must have. Why else had it only taken a few minutes? But they wouldn't tell me.

I was due to travel up to Yorkshire the next day to see the therapist I'd been referred to, but I rang my neurologist first.

'Should I go to Yorkshire?' I asked, and explained the situation.

'No, come in to see me tomorrow morning at ten to nine, before surgery starts.'

That's when I knew for sure that they'd found something. I spent the night imagining the worst and trying to talk myself round. My aunt and uncle drove me to the hospital the next morning and at my request they waited outside in the car park. I wanted to face this on my own.

'So what is it?' I asked as I sat down, more nervous than I was when I sat my O levels – and that's saying something.

The consultant looked grave. 'When I first saw you, I thought you had MS.'

I waited for the other shoe to drop.

'And it is MS.'

It's normally hard to shut me up, but I couldn't think of a single thing to say. The consultant continued that he was going to refer me for a lumbar puncture so that he could definitely rule out a couple of other things, but said he was convinced it was multiple sclerosis. He had been pretty sure from my gait when I first walked into his office, and the MRI scan had backed up his instinct. We made an appointment to talk again after I'd had the lumbar puncture.

I left his office and walked back down to the car park, where my aunt and uncle were waiting, and still I couldn't speak. I got into the car and stared at them wordlessly with an overwhelming sense that my life had just changed for ever.

Then I rejected it. He had to be wrong. Please, God, he simply had to be.

Chapter 3

'Can I Scuba-Dive?'

The only thing I knew about multiple sclerosis was that it was not a good illness to have. All I could think of was a poster I'd seen of a girl with her spine torn out and the legend 'She wishes she could walk away from this picture too.' Did that mean I wouldn't be able to walk any more? That's when I began to get upset. I couldn't bear it if I ended up in a wheelchair.

I was in a complete state when I rang my best friend, Vera, a Viking from Oslo. 'My life is over,' I wailed. 'Omar won't want to go out with me any more. No man will. My friends won't want to be my friends any more because I'll be stuck at home and I won't be able to go out. No one will want to know me. I'll be useless.' I must have sounded shrill and tearful.

Vera listened to my rant and then breathed deeply. I could feel her shifting her position to give the verbal equivalent of the slap you deliver to a hysterical woman.

'You idiot! You can't think very much of your friends if you think that. If I told you I had MS, would you stop being my friend?'

'No, but—'

'Well, how dare you even think I would stop being your friend just because you've got some disease! You wouldn't abandon me, so why would I abandon you? Stop wallowing in it. Grow up and get on with your life!'

I felt myself start. The result was pretty much as if she had indeed delivered a heavy slap: the shock brought me back to reality. This wasn't a romantic game, it was reality, and I was going to have to get used to it. I don't like to admit it, but if things are out of my control I have a tendency towards self-pity. If anything was going to drive people away, it would be that, not the diagnosis. I rang a few of my more pragmatic friends to sound them out. I didn't want people who would gush with sympathy. I wanted facts.

'Don't worry,' one friend told me. 'They've got a cure for it now.' A drug called beta-interferon had been all over the news recently. 'If you start taking it early enough, it's got a really high success rate.'

How long had I had the disease, though? When had I first noticed my legs were getting weaker? Lots of memories flooded my brain. I thought back to when I was learning to waterski in Hong Kong in 1988, seven years earlier, and I hadn't been able to stand up in the water. We'd tried over and over again, but I hadn't been able to rise elegantly from the water, so I'd sat on a jetty and they'd towed me off from there. I remember feeling frustrated. Had that been an early symptom of MS, or was it just me being clumsy and impatient? (My MS has probably been unfairly blamed for many failings

over the years, but if I've got to put up with the disease I may as well.)

I phoned other friends. Some told me they knew people with MS whose lives were barely affected. They still walked, held down jobs, had children and you'd never know they were ill except that they occasionally got a bit tired. That was comforting – that's what I wanted to hear. I'd hoped it was a brain tumour because I'd imagined that, once treated, I'd get back to my normal self without any further repercussions, but I reckoned I could cope with a mild dose of MS that was controlled by taking this new miracle-drug, beta-interferon.

I phoned my old friend Mike. He was living in Vienna but happened to be in Paris, and he said, 'Come out for the weekend. We'll take your mind off things.'

We strolled along the Seine, stopping for coffee whenever my legs got tired and I started staggering. Passersby gave me scathing looks, thinking I was drunk, and I wondered if this was something I'd have to get used to.

'Hello? Since when have you worried about what other people think?' Mike teased.

In the evenings we went to piano bars and listened to *chanteuses* singing of unfaithful lovers and lost chances. It was good to be in another place, distracted from what was going to happen to me in the coming week, never mind the coming years. Mike had just broken up with his partner, the mother of his son, so we talked about that at length and didn't dwell on my diagnosis. The only advice he gave me was about practical things, like making sure I had the insurance policy on my mortgage on my Bradford house sorted out before the diagnosis was official. Did I even have an insurance policy? I hadn't a clue.

'Are your savings in a high-interest, easy-access account?' he asked.

'What savings?' Didn't he know me at all? I wasn't the kind of girl who had savings. I lived for today, spending every penny as I earned it and sometimes even before.

Still, I pretended to take note of all Mike's nuggets of wisdom. It was good to focus on hard facts rather than speculate about the disease, and I was glad he was taking this approach and not smothering me in sympathy.

On Monday morning, after my weekend in Paris, I flew back into Gatwick Airport at 9 a.m. and jumped on a train straight to the hospital, only making it on time for my lumbar-puncture appointment because of the one-hour time difference between France and England.

The procedure was straightforward. I lay on my side on a hospital bed and curled up in a foetal position so that the doctor could stick a needle into my spine and extract some spinal fluid for testing. I was fine for the rest of the day, but the following morning I woke early feeling like I had the worst hangover of my life, with a God-awful, teeth-grinding headache that lasted for days. (I don't object to a hangover if I deserve it, but this was just unfair.) Not everyone reacts like this to lumbar punctures, I hasten to add. More than 80 per cent of patients feel fine afterwards. Just my luck to be in the wrong percentage.

I made up a list of questions to take to my next appointment with the consultant a few days later and tried to compose myself. I wanted to come across as intelligent and able, the kind of person he would be glad to have as a patient. I wouldn't break down or become hysterical; I'd be rational, logical and calm.

'Are you absolutely sure it's MS?' I asked first, a germ of hope still lingering that he might have got it wrong. 'Isn't there anything else it could be?'

'I could see the scleroses in your MRI and the lumbar puncture confirmed that it wasn't anything else,' he said.

'What are "scleroses"?' I hoped this wasn't a dumb question.

'Your central nervous system is like the wiring in your house. All electric cables have plastic round them to make sure that when you switch on an appliance the current just goes down the wire from the mains to the appliance. If you have a break in that plastic coating, the current leaks out and the appliance doesn't work.'

I nodded. That made sense so far.

'In the central nervous system the equivalent of the plastic surround is a fatty tissue called myelin. When there is damage to the myelin, it's called a sclerosis. This disease is called multiple sclerosis because there are several places where the myelin has degenerated.'

'How many?'

'Different people have different degrees of the disease. If they just have a few small scleroses in unimportant areas, they might never notice any symptoms. If they have big scleroses in important areas, they will have more problems.'

'Like not being able to walk?'

'Like not being able to walk.'

I took a deep breath. 'So what are my scleroses like?'

'Not too bad. We'll just have to wait and see how things progress.'

That was something. At least he hadn't said, 'Huge, gigantic, massive.'

'I've heard about this drug beta-interferon. Should I start taking it straight away?'

'I'm afraid you're not a suitable candidate for beta-interferon,' he said, dashing one of my pet hopes. 'There's a type of MS called relapsing-remitting and research suggests this drug may reduce the frequency of relapses, but I think you have another type called primary progressive. You've shown a pattern of mild but continuous symptoms, rather than severe episodes followed by periods of remission.'

'Is that better?' I wanted to ask, but didn't. I had a feeling it wasn't. I didn't like the sound of the word 'progressive'. Instead I asked, 'What's going to happen?'

'Debbie, the only thing I can tell you is that it's not going to get any better. That's pretty much it.' He was watching me closely for a reaction, but I was too busy weighing up his words and trying to read causes for optimism into them. 'Get on with everything you want to do whenever you want to do it, and when you find you can't do something, just stop.'

'OK,' I said cautiously.

'Meanwhile I think we should measure you for a walking stick to help broaden your base.'

What? My base is broad enough as it is, thank you. (Like I said, my bottom just can't be disguised, but people don't have to comment!)

The neurologist obviously saw my confused expression. 'I mean to steady your walking,' he replied, smiling. 'You're dragging your left foot a bit.'

My walking was particularly wobbly because I'd sprained my ankle navigating some uneven ground with Mildred's partner just before I left Singapore. We'd gone out walking in a quest for fitness and had ended up having to take a taxi home after my stumble. The episode seemed ridiculous now.

'OK,' I said. I hadn't realised you needed to be measured for walking sticks, but apparently you did.

'Any more questions?' he asked, leaning back to indicate he had all day if I needed, even though I knew he had a bulging waiting room outside.

So I took a deep breath and asked the Big One: 'There's no cure, is there?'

'No, there's no cure.'

We sat in silence for a while, my mind blank. I knew there were dozens of questions I should be asking, but I couldn't think of them and the list I'd made lay forgotten in my pocket. I decided I had better let him get on with his day, so I stood up, shook his hand and turned to leave.

I was halfway through the door when I turned back.

'Can I scuba-dive?' I asked, thinking about my job on the adventure travel brochures.

'I don't know. Can you?' he replied.

It took me a few more days to process and digest all the information he had given me because it was just so contrary to what I'd expected. I'd had a good life and thought of myself as a lucky person. Suddenly things were running away from me, escalating out of my control. I'd been expecting to be diagnosed with something serious but curable, not some incurable illness that would just keep plodding on relentlessly. I wanted something glamorous with bells and whistles. I wanted miracle-drugs and dramatic surgical interventions and cutting-edge medical breakthroughs.

'This is it, the end of my life,' I sobbed to my sister Carolyn. 'It's going to get worse and worse and then I'll die.'

'Stop being so histrionic,' she told me. 'The doctor might have got it wrong. Even if he's right, there's bound to be something that can be done. We'll just find out what it is and we'll do it.'

Although they're very different personalities, all my siblings reacted in much the same way. My brother, Stephen, was typically matter-of-fact: 'Right, OK, let's get on with things, then. No point making a fuss.'

The neurologist had said it was incurable. How was that possible? If my dad were still alive, I knew he would have found a cure. He'd been an incredible character. Thrown out of school at the age of 13 because he had a tendency to question the 'correctness' of his textbooks rather than spouting the answers teachers wanted to hear, he made a career out of his questioning mind. He was working as a photo-journalist for the Brighton News Agency when he was asked to look after a friend's typesetting business while he was on holiday. Dad thought there had to be a better way of setting type rather than placing each letter by hand. Other people had tried, but they hadn't been able to create the right size or shape of cathode-ray tube (the things that make televisions work). Dad didn't have any qualifications in electronics, and he hadn't read the books that would have told him that it wasn't possible to manufacture a tube of the size he wanted, so he just went ahead and made the right size of tube and used it to build the Linotron 505, which was the first commercially viable cathode-ray-tube typesetting machine.

He'd always been creative. Back at the age of 13, just before he was thrown out of school, he thought of a way of improving the mechanism of wind-up gramophones and wrote to HMV to tell them about it. He got a letter by return saying they had already done it, but they were impressed by his initiative and invited him to work for them. Sadly, he had to decline on the grounds that he was just a schoolboy.

Dad had tremendous enthusiasm for a challenge, as I have, and would work on one project for a few years and take it as far as he could before moving on to the next thing. After some years working as a photo-journalist, photographer and ice-cream maker, he found his *raison d'être* in new technologies that helped to revolutionise printing. The word 'incurable' would never have been in his vocabulary. Like Augusto and Michaela Odone, who researched and formulated a new drug called Lorenzo's Oil after their son, Lorenzo, was diagnosed with ALD (adrenoleukodystrophy, to give it its full name), my dad would have taken my MS diagnosis as a challenge. I'm convinced he would have cured me because he could make most things possible.

If Mum were still around, she would have given me a big hug and said, 'Don't worry, Debbie. We'll get through this, whatever it takes.' She was gone, though, and I had no one left to give me a mother's unconditional love.

This thought made me cry more than any other. I had to face this on my own, without parents. If my dad had still been alive, I'd have gone to stay with him in America and let him take care of me. I'd have felt more secure if I had even just one parent to fall back on. My sisters and brother were sympathetic, but they had busy lives with jobs and partners, and I didn't want to move in with them and lie on a sofa waiting for things to get worse. I had to figure out how to manage this disease on my own.

Should I stay in the UK to be near my doctors? Should I go back out to Singapore and try to carry on with life as it had been before? That seemed to be what the doctor was suggesting, but I was scared I wouldn't be able to manage on my own out there if my symptoms worsened.

And what about Omar? We'd only been dating for two weeks before I came back to the UK for my appointments. He couldn't be expected to take my problems on board. I didn't even know how I could begin to explain them to him, given the language barrier. He would still be in Jakarta, but I had a phone number for the club there, so I decided to call and attempt to explain what had happened.

First of all, I rang the Spanish Embassy in London and asked the woman who answered the phone, 'How do you say "multiple sclerosis" in Spanish?'

'*Esclerosis múltiple*,' she told me. (So glad I got that sorted!)

Then I rang Omar and tried to tell him, in our usual mishmash of languages, what was wrong.

'*Je suis malade. Esclerosis múltiple.*'

I was crying and I hadn't a clue what he was saying or even whether he had understood, but the calmness of his tone was comforting.

'*No te preocupes.* Come back to Singapore.'

'OK,' I sniffed. I'd had a look at the flights and there was a cheap one available on 3 April, so I told him I would get that.

'See you at Fabrice's!' I said, hoping he would pick up on the name and understand what I meant.

When I walked through the arrivals gate at Changi Airport expecting to be met by my boss, Peter, there was Omar standing waiting for me. I've never been so pleased to see anyone in my life. I ran into his arms and hugged him tightly, so relieved I couldn't speak. It was a wonderful, euphoric feeling. But what was he doing there? How had he known which flight I was on? I hadn't mentioned it to Mildred and he didn't know Peter.

Peter arrived and was able to translate for us. Although he'd grown up in Germany, he and his mother were Russian, and Omar spoke Russian, so they could communicate much more easily than Omar and I could. It seems Omar had got to the airport first thing that morning and had met every single incoming flight until I arrived after lunch.

I hugged him again, overwhelmed by my emotions.

I'd been planning to stay with Peter and his partner for a while. I wasn't sure how much work I'd be able to do, but staying with Peter would make it easier to try. I figured I'd stay in Singapore long enough to pick up my things, and maybe enjoy the city a little before having to make proper plans about my life! The immediate plan was that Peter would drive me to my flat to pick up my stuff, then take me back to his place.

When this was translated for Omar, he said not to be ridiculous. He insisted that I was to move in with him and the band. He was squeezing my hand as he spoke and looking very serious.

'*Vente a vivir con nosotros – conmigo,*' he insisted.

I thought about it for two seconds, then smiled at him and said, 'OK!'

Peter grinned.

We picked up my belongings and drove to Jalan Lada Puteh, or Peppertree Lane, where Omar lived in a house with the three girls and six boys who were members of the band.

My parachute had opened. Omar was going to take the weight.

Chapter 4

My Beautiful Career

After leaving school I led a nomadic lifestyle, never staying in one place for long. My short attention span and love of adventure meant that once I felt I'd experienced a situation, I was ready to move on. This quality used to get me into trouble back at school and college, but after the MS diagnosis I felt grateful for it. Sometimes when fear and grief for my lost life got too much, I would hide in bed, pull the covers right up over my head and cry. I'd sob my heart out, feeling desperate and helpless, but then I'd hear a story on the News Channel (it's been permanently on in my bedroom for years, only turned off at night if Omar is at home) that would make me gulp back the tears. It's hard to feel devastated by your problems with walking when you can see the effects of the tsunami in Southeast Asia, people caught in the wreckage of Hurricane Katrina or bombs dropping on Gaza. The footage of those disasters showed people in unimaginable situations dealing with their lives as best they could, and I guess it put my problems into perspective. I could turn on the tap and get fresh, clean water to take my prescription painkillers, just phone a friend for a chat or use the computer to contact friends further afield. I will always need to mourn the 'me' that I've lost, but the desperate face of a mum who has lost her child to the war in Iraq makes me so grateful for the 'me' I've still got and not want to miss out on the things I can do.

My schoolteachers always used to complain that I didn't apply myself, and none of them would have been surprised that by the age of 30 I'd done umpteen different jobs but never had what you might call a 'proper career'. I took A levels in maths, economics, government and politics, and sociology, because since the age of 13 I had wanted to be prime minister. (I took maths because I was good at it and figured it would be useful if, as prime minister, I could at least balance a chequebook.) There were always lively political discussions at the dinner table at home, and with the arrogance of youth I thought I could solve the world's problems by making the political system more fair and inclusive. I joined the Liberal Party and committed a lot of time and energy to the causes I believed would improve the world – as well as the ones that looked most fun.

I spent a couple of years knocking on doors campaigning for local councillors, and I learned wheelchair basketball and helped out at Sports Association for the Disabled. I planned to change the world by improving my corner of it. However, the more I learned about society, the more I realised that tweaking the existing status quo would be harder and less effective than building a new one. I began to read more political literature, and the more I read the more I considered myself a Marxist.

I took two of my A levels at a further-education college in Windsor. I remember my time there mainly for that first parachute jump with the Territorial Army, back in 1981, sparking my lifelong addiction to adrenaline rushes. About fifty of us, male and female, had signed up for the jump. During a couple of days away from college, I thought better of it and returned planning to drop out, but I discovered that of our original fifty, only six remained, all of them boys. That made me the last girl standing and I felt I had to do it as a matter of feminist principle.

I moved to London to do my other two A levels at a college near Old Street, and I lived in a squat – rather a nice squat, an old vicarage – with a fantastic bunch of people: a city stockbroker, a Buddhist with a motley collection of stray cats and, the reason I was there, some Marxist revolutionaries. I learned a lot, not least about choosing the battles that were most important and not being sidetracked by every little injustice you perceive. I went to Kingston Polytechnic to study sociology. Then, after a term and a half, I moved to Birmingham to read humanities (economics, politics and sociology). I made the move to Birmingham because of politics rather than education (although I think my involvement in politics was the best education available). I worked a few nights a week as a nightclub hostess, greeting people at the door and checking they conformed to the dress code (on the way in, anyway), and if we had live bands on, we had to frisk people if they looked suspicious.

In Birmingham, I decided that I wouldn't graduate. I thought I was learning more from living, arguing and listening than I was from lectures. I bought my first house in Lozells, Birmingham, back in the days of 100 per cent mortgages, when buying was cheaper than renting. My bank manager said I should definitely go for a job selling advertising space for Thomson Directories because I had convinced him to lend me the £11,000 for the house while still a student! (These were the days when houses were homes, not investments.)

Nowadays you need a degree to become a toilet cleaner, but in the 1980s you didn't, and when a man I met at the club offered me a job selling advertising space it seemed like a good idea. The money was better than a student grant (a historical anachronism), and although I'd had many jobs since the age of 14 – including working in a farm shop, plucking Christmas turkeys, mucking out stables and working as a hospital cleaner – this would be the first real one. It seemed about time I had a job that meant I'd stay clean, warm and dry, and that I needed to dress properly for.

I was something of a fashion victim in those days, but the phases never lasted very long. I was punk for a week or so, but found the look too uncomfortable and got impatient with the amount of time it took to get ready in the morning. For a while I had a short back and sides with tufts of different-coloured hair – orange and blue and pink – and I'd wear tight little black dresses, making me look like a parakeet.

I started the telesales job in Birmingham, but when some friends were moving to Edinburgh I went too and found a field sales job for the *Scotsman*. Then, within a year, I got a job with Yellow Pages. I loved the variety of working as a field sales rep: at 9 a.m. I could be at the stylish offices of a multinational corporation, at 10.30 in a draughty barn talking to a farmer about his plant-hire sideline, and at noon I might be at a local tanning salon. I met loads of wonderful people and travelled all over Scotland and the north of England, feeling energised by my life and the people in it. Even so, I still found myself hankering after change.

My dad had been working a lot in the United States for most of the last decade, leaving my mum at home in Britain, but in 1985 he took a contract in Oslo. The following year I decided to go out and stay with him for a while. We'd only seen each other sporadically while he was in America and I missed him. We spoke on the phone, but it wasn't the same as being part of each other's lives. In fact, on arrival, I realised there was a rather major piece of news he hadn't shared with me – a girlfriend called Eppy, who had two kids, aged about 12 and 15. He had never mentioned this part of his life and I was surprised, to say the least.

The night I arrived in Norway, Dad took me to stay with some Norwegian friends so he could explain to me about his living arrangements on neutral territory. He wasn't sure how I would react, but he told me that his marriage to Mum had been unhappy (what a surprise!) and that he had been with Eppy for several years. The children were hers, not his. I was sad that he hadn't been able to share this with his children sooner. Despite his free-thinking scientific brain, he was still conditioned by society to keep up a pretence and avoid admitting that his marriage had failed.

I must be jinxed! Not long after I arrived, the company Dad was working with went out of business, so he wasn't needed and returned to the States. I loved it in Norway, even in winter temperatures of minus 20 degrees, and I decided to stay. I got a job selling jewellery on a market stall, which turned out to be virtually the only stall in the area that had a licence to trade. There were dozens of illegal stalls, and when the police came by, everyone would quickly load their goods under my stall and disappear.

Lots of different nationalities lived side by side – Palestinians, French, Algerians, Germans, Americans – selling jewellery, trinkets and dodgy records. There was a great community feeling. The Norwegian company Dad had worked with had paid the lease on his house for almost another year, so I stayed on when he left and shocked the neighbours by letting a few of my bohemian friends move in. One of them taught me to ski, which I took to straight away. Living in Oslo was fantastic. Great cross-country or downhill ski runs were only a short bus, tram or boat ride from the city. To me, getting there was as much fun as being there. They weren't flashy slopes with smart restaurants and multiple chairlifts, like you find in the fashionable resorts in the Alps – just clean, family-oriented spaces. That didn't cost anything.

A girl I met while working on the jewellery stall took me to the Café de Paris one night and I immediately loved the friendly atmosphere. The owners were a Norwegian-Algerian woman and her French husband, both of whom treated the club like an extension of their home, rather than a place of business, and it worked. It had such a warm, welcoming atmosphere, and it was a second home for a lot of foreigners – French-speaking Africans, African-Americans from the NATO base and of course a wide-eyed English girl. When they offered me a job behind the bar, I decided to accept. I continued working on my jewellery stall by day and took up residence behind the bar of the Café de Paris by night. If they hadn't paid me to be there, I would have spent all my money on the other side of the bar. It was home-from-home and my time there would prove to be one of those rare life-changing experiences because I met loads of people who would become friends for life: my best friend Vera, Greg (the friend who was with me the day I collapsed in Bradford), Chris Merchant, who was an English singer, the American club manager Dwayne, and Mildred Jones, the singer who eventually coaxed me to Singapore.

Meeting Mildred for the first time was kind of scary. She was larger than life at over 6 feet tall, yet she wore vertiginous high heels, glamorous dresses covered in seed pearls and glitter, full make-up and long lacquered nails – and that was just for breakfast! On stage she was a colossus: incredibly imposing, oozing sex appeal and with the voice of a diva. During her long career, which started in the late 1950s, she had been instrumental in encouraging clubs to open their doors to black artists. She had toured Russia with B. B. King and had played all over Scandinavia, as well as in her native America. She wrote her own songs, full of *double entendres*, and always had love-struck admirers milling around. She was in her 50s by the time I met her and didn't encourage these men (some very young). I once overheard her say, 'Honey, I've got underwear that's older than you!' But they were like flies to flypaper.

When Omar first met Mildred, he thought she must be a man, due to her stature and deep voice. Singapore was home to lots of lady-boys and it took me a long time to convince him that she was 100 per cent woman under the seed pearls and glitter. Too much woman for most men to handle.

Mildred was playing in the piano bar at the Grand Hotel, just down the road from the Café de Paris. She was usually starving when she finished her set at 1 a.m., so Dwayne would send up a plate of food covered in silver foil. It became my job to take up her late-night supper, and when she noticed that I had fake nails too, she asked if I would come back the next day to help repair hers: she would batter them nightly on the piano and nail salons were crazy money. My hand was trembling the first time I squeezed out the little blobs of glue and positioned the nails in place, but somehow they didn't go wonky, so I acquired another (unpaid) job. I was in awe of her for ages, until I got comfortable with the astonishing presence and came to appreciate that beneath the glitz she was a down-to-earth southern belle with a filthy sense of humour and a raucous laugh.

Greg was a drop-dead gorgeous American who worked for NATO, and we nicknamed him 'GQ' because he was always so impeccably dressed. I dated him briefly, but it's weird going out with someone who has more hair products than you and takes much longer to get ready to go out in the evening. We drifted easily into friendship and I lived platonically in his flat with him for a couple of months when I needed somewhere to stay.

Vera was working behind the bar in the Café de Paris the first week I was there. I heard it was her birthday and I took a cake from the pantry, but I couldn't find any candles, so I stuck in a light bulb with 'Happy Birthday' scrawled on it. I left it in the fridge for her to find and she thought it was funny. We just clicked. Like me, she loved travelling and music (she plays piano beautifully) and, of course, men. Unfortunately her taste was a bit dodgy in those days and she fell for the club doorman.

Despite (or rather because of) the fact that we were the only girls working at the Café de Paris, at one time Dwayne, who was a gay, black American, used to make us do all the heavy work. He said he didn't want to risk injuring one of 'his boys' and would get our names mixed up. When it was pointed out what our names were, he'd dismiss us with an imperious wave, saying, 'You all look the same to me.' He was wonderfully eccentric, very stylish, always strutting around in a long, flapping coat and Cuban heels, and I absolutely loved working with him.

I stayed in Oslo for a couple of years, longer than I had stayed anywhere in my adult life at that point, but then things began to change at the Café de Paris as my friends upped and moved. Mildred had gone back to her hometown of Houston,

Texas, and she called and invited me to work there with her for a while. She said she needed someone to help her sort out the copyright on her songs. I reckoned I could manage that, and of course I wanted to see more of the States. My dad was living there again, so I'd be able to squeeze in a visit to see him and Eppy (whose real name, I found out, was Ethel).

I spent a few months with Mildred in Houston, learning some facts about the music world that would stand me in good stead later on, and I grew to love Americans. After leaving Texas, I planned to continue westwards round the world to visit my uncle Tony, who was working in Hong Kong. The plane had to stop briefly in Tokyo, and though I very much wanted to see the city, the cost of breaking my flight was prohibitive, so it was straight on to Hong Kong. When we landed in Tokyo, though, an announcement was made. It seemed the plane was over-booked, so they wanted to know if anyone would be willing to stay the night in Japan, all expenses paid, plus $200. Of course my hand shot up at lightning speed. The next day was the same, and the one after that. I was staying in a much nicer hotel than I could afford, with all my meals paid for, and by now I had received more in compensation than my ticket had cost. By the time they had space on the onward flight, I'd met some people and been offered a job dancing in Tokyo's Roppongi district, so I decided to stay for a while.

The men I came across were very respectful. I loved dancing and European girls did well in those bars, where if you had even the slightest bit of rhythm they thought you were Janet Jackson.

By day I had a few jobs making conversation in English with Japanese businessmen so they could polish up their language skills. I lived well enough, sharing a flat with another girl, but after about seven months I felt it was time to go. The wanderlust took over and it was off again, this time to Hong Kong.

I arrived to find that Uncle Tony wasn't there any more, but on my very first night I went to the bar of a hotel where I planned to stay and there was Chris, the English singer I'd met in Oslo. I stayed with him and his wife while I looked for a job and found my feet.

A girl called Jane, who had been working with my uncle Tony before he left Hong Kong, helped me find a job. While looking though her photo album after dinner one night, I was stunned to see a photo of my ex-flatmate Joss, with whom I'd lived for a while. We compared notes and realised I had taken Jane's old room when I moved in with Joss.

I did a couple of different jobs in Hong Kong. Jane introduced me to an ad agency based in the building where she worked, and I started working for them selling corporate sponsorship for a road-safety project called Constable Care. I had more time (and enthusiasm) than anyone else in the company, so ended up running it. Because of the experience I gained there of bringing together the Government Information Services (GIS), the police, army, kids with corporate sponsors and the media, I ended up helping Ogilvy & Mather PR set up and run the Keep Hong Kong Clean campaign. (The first taught me the power of the media, the second to deal with failure.)

When I'd got myself settled, Vera came over to join me from Oslo and she moved into my flat for a few months. She was now studying sociology and managed to get a grant. We figured that living in Hong Kong and reading her textbooks would probably be good study. The exchange rate and difference in the cost of living meant she could get by in Hong Kong for the academic year.

It was a brilliant place to live, with 24-hour music and parties. It was obsessed with money and hedonism, probably a bit like the City in London but with a better climate.

I lived in Hong Kong from 1988 to the end of 1990, and I was there when the students protested in Tiananmen Square and Chinese troops opened fire on them. Information wasn't getting through to the Chinese public, who didn't have access to Western media, so the *South China Morning Post* printed cut-out A4 pages explaining the situation and anyone who could faxed them to contacts on the mainland. The massacre caused consternation in Hong Kong because the 1997 handover had already been arranged and was fast approaching and locals were worried that this might be the way they would be treated under Chinese rule.

Meanwhile, back home, Mum's health had been deteriorating over the years and she was now finding it difficult to look after herself. She was overweight, and that probably contributed to her lack of mobility, but it was also the reason why she wouldn't ever consult doctors. 'They'll only tell me to lose weight,' she complained, and I'm sure she was right. Unfortunately it meant that her diabetes was never diagnosed.

Uncle Frank, the husband of Mum's sister Beryl, was diabetic, so Mum would clip recipes out of magazines that would be suitable for him, while still eating sugary foods herself. She didn't complain much about her health, but she needed someone to help her with shopping and housework and anything that required much energy. Carolyn had been doing it for years, and I now felt it was time I helped.

I flew back from 25° sunshine to cold, grey, rainy Bradford, a city I'd never lived in before and where I knew no one apart from Mum and Carolyn. I got a job in Leeds with a recruitment agency, Michael Page. I initially went to ask them to find me a job, but they laughed and offered me a job with them instead. I bought a house near Mum's, a tall, narrow terrace on a steep hill. Mum was happy to have me at home, and I was happy to be able to spend time with her. I was nearly 27 years old and had had more than a dozen careers to date, so maybe it was time for me to settle down just a bit.

I really enjoyed getting close to Mum again, but we were to have limited time together because in 1992, just over a year after I came back to Britain, she died very suddenly. The shock left me reeling for the next couple of years. I couldn't decide what to do with myself any more. I felt unbalanced, like a tree without roots or a house without foundations.

Dad came back and took a job in Cheltenham. I took a marketing job in Redditch, near Birmingham, and was able to live with him during the week and drive back to Bradford at weekends. The work was fine at first, but I soon got frustrated. When you keep changing profession, as I did, you never get a chance to work your way up to the interesting jobs at the top. No one's going to offer you a massive new opportunity when you have a track record like mine. Some people stay with the same employer for decades and climb the ladder – my brother worked for the BBC for over twenty years – but it wasn't in my nature to put my head down and work. So when Mildred rang and invited me out to Singapore in September 1994, I was ready to change jobs, homes, continents, everything.

Within a week of arriving, Mildred had introduced me to Peter and I'd got the job with Adventure Travel, a company that offered adrenaline-fuelled package breaks to expats living throughout the Far East. They needed someone who knew where the apostrophes should go and I persuaded them that punctuation was my specialist subject.

The job was like a dream come true for me, especially when Peter said he'd like me to go and check out some of the sporting activities and write copy myself – except that my MS diagnosis came only a few months after I'd started. Would I still be able to do all the things they needed me to? I was utterly determined that nothing would stand between me and my newfound love of scuba-diving, so in April 1995, soon after I returned to Singapore, I went to review an Indonesian dive site.

I could still swim and breathe in the mask, so I didn't think there would be a problem. After a dive one day, though, I swam to the shore and was walking up the beach when I looked down and saw I'd left a trail of bloody footprints all the way up the sand. My feet had been cut to ribbons on the sharp coral and I hadn't felt a thing. That was a bit of a shock. I was going to have to take a little more care of myself.

Peter sent me on a number of other trips: white-water rafting down rapids on the edge of a jungle in Borneo and more scuba-diving, but I learned to keep an eye on my legs because I couldn't trust that I was feeling sensations in them accurately. They weren't responding the way I'd been used to. I never thought I'd be doing this job for too long, but I'd figured a bit longer than this.

Writing about music gave me the chance to meet and interview lots of fascinating people, and gave me free access to Singapore's buzzing music scene, but the late nights were becoming harder to cope with (even before my MS diagnosis).

My next job – one I'm still doing today, albeit a bit differently – was managing Omar. It's not something I actively chose in the beginning, but I was living with a houseful of musicians. Their talent lay in making music and mine lay in organisation, so we all just did what we could. They also each did what they could to make my life easier (except getting places on time).

It was incredible luck that I met Omar and the Cuban Boys when I did. The timing was impeccable. They needed managing and they met me, and I became friends with a bunch of people who were able to make me laugh at things that would otherwise have made me cry. It was through them that I worked out how to deal with the disease. Because of them, I was able to take my neurologist's advice and get on with everything I wanted to do for as long as I could.

Chapter 5

The Boys from Cuba

The house where the Cuban Boys were living in Singapore had five bedrooms to accommodate the ten of them. Omar had been sharing a room with Mariano, the bass player. After I moved in, Mariano would stay elsewhere whenever he could to give Omar and me some space. No one seemed to mind my arrival. It was a very easy place to live. We took it in turns to shop and clean up and cook, although there was only really breakfast to worry about because the band could eat dinner at a restaurant owned by Fabrice (as per their contract) and there really wasn't time between getting up and dinner to think about lunch.

Omar started trying to teach me Spanish so we could communicate better, but he wasn't the world's most sympathetic language teacher. If I said something that was grammatically incorrect, or mispronounced a word, he would call the rest of the band into the room and get me to repeat it and they would all fall about laughing. After the fourth or fifth time he did this, I announced, 'Right! That's it. I give up.

You'll have to learn English instead.' And I stuck to my guns. We were living in a country where English was the universal language, so it was more useful for him to learn English than for me to learn Spanish.

In a way, I didn't want to learn Spanish, because I had a feeling I didn't want to hear everything that was being said. Omar flirts with anybody and everybody, and being a nice Englishwoman, it makes me a little uncomfortable. He tells women how beautiful they are. He genuinely means it; he has never been that impressed with half-clothed nubile lovelies, but finds women intriguing. If a woman is wearing a new dress or has changed her hairstyle, he will comment on it. It doesn't mean he plans to try it on with her; he just notices and comments. I decided it was easier if I didn't know everything he was saying. Because we were together twenty-four hours a day, privacy was precious and language could provide that.

On stage the band members were charming, sexy, flirty musicians, but if I saw one of them standing straight like a lollipop stick and playing his instrument without any of the normal messing around I knew it was probably because his girlfriend was in that night. And I didn't want to be the person who turned Omar into a lollipop stick.

Of course, he didn't like anyone to flirt with me. Omar once finished his part, put down his violin, left the stage, 'encouraged' a man who was drunkenly chasing me round our table to leave, then got back on stage and picked up his violin without missing a beat.

A month after I moved back to Singapore post-diagnosis, it was my 32nd birthday. I hadn't realised that in Cuba they celebrate birthdays as the clock strikes midnight, so when Omar asked me to come to the club because they were trying something different that he wanted me to hear, I didn't think anything of it, even when he was insistent: 'Make sure you are there for the first set. We're going to do this new thing really early on.' (Of course, our conversations weren't nearly as fluent as this; they were still monosyllabic, spoken in whatever language we could remember a word and accompanied by plenty of sign language. It took us twenty minutes to have a three-sentence conversation, which is actually quite good at the beginning of a relationship because it means you can't argue.)

I obediently turned up at the club and was surprised when, in the middle of the first set, the whole band launched into a very Cuban version of 'Happy Birthday'. As the number ended, Omar climbed off stage and came over to hand me a red rose. It was a fabric rose because, he explained, he'd been running late and hadn't had time to go for a real one. The thought was so romantic. I still have the rose: I'm an old romantic too.

He continued to introduce me at gigs, after going through the band members, by saying, 'There's the woman who has my heart in chains.' Some of the other guys decided this clearly worked – if it turned the most ferocious tiger into a purring pussycat, it was worth a try – but it never worked as well as it did for Omar. Originality probably says sincerity.

Our schedules were completely different in those days. Omar got back from the club at three or four in the morning, by which time I would usually be sound asleep in bed. He'd wake me up to share the night with me. It was nice, I suppose, that he wanted to include me in everything he did, but it took hours to go back to sleep. I had to get up at nine to be at work for ten, and if I accidentally woke Omar while I was getting dressed he would complain, without any sense of irony, 'Why aren't you respecting my sleep?'

Gradually, with the help of a well-thumbed dictionary, Omar's improving English and Rolando's occasional translations, I began to learn his life history and find out more about the man I was living with.

Omar Puente was born in Santiago de Cuba in 1962, three years after the revolution that brought Fidel Castro to power. His father was a doctor, and the family had been living in New York but decided to return in 1959 because Cuba was in desperate need of doctors. After the revolution thousands of predominantly wealthy, white and Hispanic professionals left the island, fearful of what might change. Omar's parents joined thousands of Cuban expatriates going the other way. Many Afro-Cubans and native Cubans had found it difficult to practise professions under the previous Batista dictatorship. Now they went home to family and friends. In 1962 his mum and dad already had a 10-year-old son, Victor, so it must have been a shock when baby Omar put in an appearance.

Little Omar loved music from the word go and he was sent to the Esteban Salas music school in Santiago, and then, at the age of 12, he won a scholarship to the prestigious Escuela Nacional de Arte in Havana. There he was taught classical violin by the top Russian and Cuban teachers (hence he speaks some Russian) and spent his evenings hanging around Havana's famous music halls and developing a taste for Latin music. It was the heyday of Havana. Musicians like Chucho Valdés, Rubén González and Guillermo Rubalcaba were playing nightly. Omar was in his element.

In 1978 he saw the jazz fusion band Weather Report playing at Havana's Karl Marx Stadium and he left the gig on a high, thinking, I want to be able to make people feel that way one day. He loved Latin music, he loved classical, and he was developing a taste for jazz.

The family were living in an apartment near Havana's famous Malecón, where the Gulf of Mexico crashes up on to the rocks, only separated from a main road through the city by a sea wall. After the revolution, everyone got food, housing, education and healthcare, all the essentials, but the American blockade meant that if you wanted to buy international goods, like records by American artists, you needed foreign currency. Omar started playing his violin in restaurants, where tourists left foreign-currency tips, and that's where he perfected his 'charm'. The more customers liked him, the bigger the tips, so flattery and flirtation were useful talents.

When Omar left school, he was due to go to the Moscow Conservatoire to study classical music, but instead he was accepted at Cuba's newly founded Instituto Superior de Arte, which is a university for the performing arts. The teaching there was intense and he met loads of musicians with whom he would work throughout his career: Omar Sosa, a pianist who now lives in Spain; Giraldo Piloto, leader of a band called Klimax; Gonzalito Rubalcaba, the son of the famous Guillermo; and Angá Diaz, a brilliant percussionist, among others. They graduated in 1986 and each spread across the globe finding work, but always kept in touch.

When Omar was in his early 20s his beloved father died. His elder brother died shortly afterwards, following an asthma attack. At the age of 24, Omar felt it was up to him to take responsibility for his mother and support his sister-in-law, mother of two of his three nephews, Victor, Aaron and Ramses. He's a very practical person who doesn't have time for weeping and wailing and high emotion – he just gets on with things, and that's what he did.

Omar isn't a political person and he never joined the Communist Party in Cuba, but he is fiercely loyal to his country. They have a world-class education system and universal healthcare. Cubans look out for each other, as they do in all community-dominated cultures. They have a saying that I love (and try to live up to): 'We share what we have, not what we have left over.' He grew up without extreme poverty or extreme wealth. No one has much, but they all have enough.

There are lots of myths about Cuban society, one of them being that Cubans aren't allowed to travel, but Omar has been travelling as long as he's been working. (Having said that, visa requirements for Cubans make me glad I'm British.)

Cuban musicians have a tradition of gaining experience by apprenticing themselves to established musicians. Omar enjoyed apprenticeships with some of the great names in Cuban music, through which he got to tour Europe, Latin America and the Far East, while also maintaining a place in the Orquesta Sinfónica Nacional de Cuba. No wonder he could switch musical styles so seamlessly, as I'd noticed the first time I saw him playing: he'd been doing it all his life.

The Cuban Boys got together in Havana in 1992, when Omar and Rolando answered an advert that read, 'Wanted: good-looking, energetic young musicians.' Jean-Luc, a Swiss agent, was putting together a fourteen-piece band to take to the Monte Carlo Sporting Club with a repertoire of Cuban music from the 1920s up to the present day. There were singers and dancers, all wearing extravagant costumes, and they went down a storm, but the group disbanded once they returned to Cuba.

'Hey, this band is really good,' Omar said to Rolando and Juan Carlos. 'We should keep it going.' (They were speaking in Spanish, of course.)

The band leader had left and gone his own way and they needed a new one. 'Why don't you do it?' they asked Omar, and a new band was born.

At the time I first saw the Cuban Boys, in 1995, they were a fledgling group, but they already sounded tight. They had supported Whitney Houston, MC Hammer and Tony Bennett in Monte Carlo and had won a reputation for their on-stage charisma as well as their music. They were all good friends, but Omar was the leader, and although it was neither particularly natural for him nor even welcome, he took his job seriously. It was one of the qualities that attracted me to him, though he prefers to think it was his amazing good looks and charm.

The contract at Fabrice's in Singapore was beneficial for them because it was a late-night venue where other musicians hung out after they'd finished work, so was a good place to meet people. The eponymous Fabrice was a cool Belgian guy with a taste for world music, especially African and Latin. His club was in a dark basement with a dance floor and was always heaving. These were the days when the Gipsy Kings were so hot their records came with a fire warning! There was always someone in the audience who, thinking world music was a specific genre like jazz or pop, would ask an incredible African band to cover 'Bamboleo', but most of the crowd just wanted to have a good time and listen to the best music available.

Now I was living with the Cuban Boys I didn't go to hear them as much. I had my own friends to see and sometimes I was reviewing gigs in another part of town, but I would turn up whenever I could. My sprained ankle healed, but I still used a walking stick to get around because I could get wobbly when I was tired. If I had to get to the other side of town, Rolando or one of the other musicians would announce, 'Hey! I'm going that way as well.' They'd drop me off where I needed to be, and if possible someone else would pick me up later. It wasn't discussed. No one said, 'Whose turn is it to go with Debbie?' but someone often did.

I tried to do my fair share of cooking and housework and no one would stop me, but if I put the broom down in exhaustion halfway through sweeping, someone would take over. If we were out somewhere and my legs got a bit wobbly, everyone would club together to pay for a taxi home. No one was well off, but they'd throw in whatever change they had that evening until there was enough for a taxi fare. Sometimes my legs collapsed under me, as they'd done that day in Bradford, and whoever was nearest would help me to a chair or get me home to bed. My symptoms seemed to worsen when I was overheated, so if I felt bad I would go and lie on the tiled bathroom floor of our house until I cooled down.

No one made a fuss about it. We never talked about my illness. I don't think anyone (including me) understood what MS was and we didn't think of it as a serious problem. Omar certainly didn't have any idea what the progression of the disease might bring, but then neither did I. His attitude was to get on with it and deal with whatever needed to be dealt with at the time, and I appreciated the fact that he didn't make a big fuss about it. It meant I could forget that I had MS, until some intrusive symptom reminded me.

Most of the time I felt OK. I loved living in Singapore, feeling the sun on my skin, listening to great music and mixing with a huge, eclectic bunch of friends, then going home to bed with a gorgeous Cuban man. Bit by bit I was getting to know Omar better, but he still had the capacity to surprise me, and I liked that. Usually. Having said that, some surprises were more welcome than others.

Omar still called me 'Rabbit' and had lots of other pet names for me, always something sweet. It never for one second occurred to me that all those endearments were being used because he didn't actually know my name.

There is a point beyond which you can't ask the woman you are sleeping with what she is called. The morning after is probably too late, and three months after she has moved in with you is beyond the pale. Poor Omar. What was he to do?

The truth only came out one day in June 1995, when a musician we both knew came to borrow a tape from him. As he left, he said, 'If I don't see you later, I'll give it back to Debbie.'

Omar, standing on the doorstep with his arm around me, asked, 'Who's Debbie?'

We both turned to look at him in total amazement.

As if that weren't enough, there was another, even bigger surprise waiting. The Cuban Boys were playing at the Montreux Jazz Festival that July and I managed to secure a commission to write a piece about the festival for Jazz Australia, an interactive website. I was excited to be there with them and listen to all the great music. Afterwards, the band was going home to Cuba and I would fly back to Singapore to write my commission and try and find a new contract for them because the contract with Fabrice's had ended. Not long after my return I had a phone call from a girlfriend of Mariano's in Switzerland.

'Did you know that Omar is married?' she asked.

I was amazed. I thought I'd covered that, and we had been living together for months.

'He saw her recently in Italy. That's where she lives.'

I hung up, utterly devastated. He'd lied to me. Everyone had lied to me. He was married to another woman and I was his bit on the side. I'd always said I would never go out with a married man, and I wasn't about to start now.

I wasn't going to let the rest of the band down, so I decided I'd get the contract but wouldn't see Omar any more. That was the end. We'd had a good few months, and he'd helped me a lot in dealing with the initial news about my MS, but I was on my own again now. It was like a knife twisting in my gut, but I had my principles and I was damn sure I was going to stick to them. I moved into a friend's flat and slept on the sofa.

When the band landed at Singapore's Changi Airport ten days later, I wasn't there to meet them. Omar already knew he was in trouble because one of the girls had told the rest of the band about the call. I wouldn't let him into my friend's flat. I didn't want a dialogue about it. I wanted to be left alone.

Omar got every mutual friend he could think of to intervene on his behalf. They explained to me that his wife, Jamilla, had been living with someone else for a while now. They said it's very simple to get married in Cuba; it's just paperwork. Omar had been married to Jamilla for a few years, but they'd drifted apart and neither of them had yet bothered to apply for a divorce because they didn't see a need. They weren't still together. He hadn't told me because he didn't think it was important. You would think I'd understand unconventional marriages, given my parents' history.

I sent back a message that I'd try and arrange a contract for Jamilla, who was a pianist, if she wanted to be with Omar. I just didn't want to look a fool.

Omar didn't give up. I was couch-surfing, moving from one friend's to the next, but Omar kept coming round to try and talk to me. I told him that my principles didn't let me go out with married men, full stop, and he thought I was crazy. We couldn't see eye to eye at all.

On his part, he was furious that Mariano's girlfriend, who was supposed to be a friend of his, had tried to make trouble between us. It was a big shock to him to have someone he had previously liked do something so destructive. I think the idea was that if I didn't get them a contract in Singapore Mariano, at least, would go back to Switzerland. I'm not sure she thought it through.

Omar kept getting other people to try and put his point of view across to me, and gradually I softened. Had he gone to Italy to see her? He said not. I chose to believe him. It was a few months after the phone call before I moved back into Omar's house and his bed. A long, difficult period. Without him I felt as though I was facing the wrong direction and couldn't see where I was going. Once we got back together the world felt right again.

The point is, it's hard to be angry with Omar about anything. He is what he is, and most of the time he is consideration and charm personified from the soles of his feet to the top of his head. The more I got to know him, the more I realised that my instinct, the first time I watched him playing, was correct. I had judged the character of the man from the way he played his violin and the way he moved around the stage. I learned more sides to him over the coming months and years, but my first impression of someone witty, intelligent and caring remained. As I grew to know him better I realised that he was trustworthy as well. That time apart was so hard that I realised I had fallen in love with the man. Otherwise I wouldn't have gone back to him.

Still he hadn't told me he loved me. We never talked about our relationship. Maybe this was all just casual for him. Perhaps I really was his bit on the side, as I'd thought when I first got the phone call about Jamilla.

One night we were walking home from the club. There was a steep flight of stairs to climb and I got tired near the top, so we sat down on a step to let me rest awhile. The sky was a dark bluey-purple, with a gleaming crescent moon, the city spread out below us in a wash of hazy orange and pink and yellow lights, and my emotions finally boiled over.

'Omar, maybe we should think about calling it a day because you obviously aren't in love with me, not the way that Rolando cares for Isabella.' I then listed a string of friends of ours who were ostentatious about their feelings. How come those girls received all the extravagant compliments and romantic endearments while I didn't get any?

Omar said quietly, 'I can tell you I love you, or I can show you.'

I realised then that he was showing me simply by being there, sitting on a step in the middle of the night with a girl

71

who had MS and was too tired to walk home. I didn't need pretty words and gushing affection. I needed him to be exactly the way he was.

Chapter 6

'My Missus'

Being surrounded by a group of people who didn't know anything about multiple sclerosis was the ideal thing for me in the first couple of years after I was diagnosed. No one made a big deal of it; no one asked me questions about it; none of us knew what to be frightened of. I wasn't looking ahead and anticipating what might happen next – I was just living for now.

When symptoms arose, I found ways to deal with them. When I found that my vision became more blurred when I drank coffee, I gave up coffee. I found it was happening with tea as well – a big problem for an English girl – and I figured hot drinks were the problem and gave them up completely. If I walked too far I got wobbly, so I planned my life so that I didn't have to walk far. If I did too much swimming, my vision got so bad I couldn't even see the end of the pool, so I restricted myself to a couple of lengths. Simple. I could still do most of the Adventure Travel sports I was sent to cover. Scuba-diving was fine in short bursts; I just couldn't be someone's buddy. (You dive in pairs to watch each other. It's called the buddy system.) I could still earn a little by writing, and fortunately I didn't need much, with Omar supporting me at home and regular flights between England and Singapore negotiated into his contracts.

Every couple of months I flew over to England to see my family and check in with my doctors. They did a few physical tests on me, but there was nothing they could do to halt the progression of the disease and we all knew it. We talked about the symptoms I was experiencing and the deterioration in my walking. The distances I could manage were getting shorter, and my exhaustion after any kind of physical exertion was increasing. I'd had a few falls and I was worried about breaking bones or cracking my head, although so far all I'd incurred were some nasty bruises.

'Why don't we get you a wheelchair?' the doctor suggested. 'A folding one that you can use when you need it.'

My immediate reaction was to say, 'No, I don't want one.' It felt as though I would be giving in and becoming an invalid, but when I thought about it I realised how useful it would be. If someone could push me up steep hills, or if we had any distance to cover, it would save a lot of money on taxi fares. It would be good to have that option, even if I didn't use it much. I certainly didn't plan to use it every day, or anything like it. It was just a temporary measure for use in emergencies only, while I was staying in Asia.

The boys in the band thought my wheelchair was fantastic! They borrowed a bicycle from someone and soon they were zipping around the parking area outside our house having chariot races across the big loose cobblestones. I seldom used that chair myself – it was just a new toy for my housemates to play with.

In November 1995 the band was moving to Kuala Lumpur for a three-month contract, so I went along. We had a nice house in a residential district, but it was miles from the centre and the neighbours weren't very understanding about the noise a bunch of Cubans could make when they came home from a gig at three in the morning. I tried to stop them playing their instruments at that hour, but even a game of dominos could be noisy as they slapped them down on the table Caribbean-style and yelled in frustration if they were losing.

The neighbours spoke English, so they came to me to complain and by default I became the one responsible for trying to keep the noise down.

'That's too loud!'

'No, it's not.'

'It's seven in the morning.'

'I'm just playing some music.'

Omar's English was coming along well by this time. It had to, since I had stuck to my resolution not to learn Spanish. Of course, the downside of his newfound eloquence was that we were now able to argue, and we did. I'm English in my style of arguing, so I was totally unprepared for the way he would blow up, let off steam, then forget about the whole thing immediately afterwards. I was too reserved to scream and shout back at him, so I would sulk instead. Omar doesn't believe in holding a grudge and wasn't about to let me do so. While I was lying in bed with my back to him after an argument, he would take out his violin and start playing. There was no way I could carry on sulking after that. It wasn't his way of saying sorry, mind you. (He's a man and would never admit to being in the wrong.) He was just saying, 'Let's agree to differ,' in his own special way.

Gradually I came round to his arguing style and learned to blow my top and let it all out with the best of them, but we always made up again immediately. We never went to bed on an argument or stormed out of the house. We got into a habit that we had to make up before he headed off for a gig in the evening, or before travelling anywhere without the other, and it was a good habit to have.

Most arguments were about trivial things, such as time-keeping. If a Latin man says he'll be there at 6.30, you can guarantee he'll get there at 10. The band's old agent, Jean-Luc, was based in Switzerland, so I had taken over all the arrangements for them regarding transport and plane tickets and the timing of gigs. The band was happy for me to do it, because they could focus on being creative, but it was a nightmare for me, mainly because of their laid-back attitudes towards punctuality.

They might say they would be there at 8.30, and at the time they said it they fully intended to be there at 8.30, but when something else came along that diverted their attention it wouldn't occur to them to let me know. It was the same as declaring undying love to a girl one minute and meaning it at the time, then forgetting her when she was out of sight. Their attention was focused on the present, the here and now.

'Omar, you're going to be late. You've got to get moving.'

'I'm gonna be there.'

'No, you're not. Not unless you can fly.'

I got fed up trying to shepherd them all through the door like a clucking mother hen, then apologising for their lateness when we reached our destination, but that's part and parcel of the job when you manage a band of Latin musicians. It would always be that way.

One of the biggest arguments Omar and I had was in Kuala Lumpur in late 1995 and was about another kind of cultural difference entirely. We were friendly with lots of staff members from the South African Embassy in the city. South Africans feel an affinity with Cubans because Cuba had long supported the African National Congress (ANC) in their fight against apartheid in the region. The embassy officials invited us to a South African restaurant one night and I was horrified to see 'elephant steaks' on the menu.

'What's the problem?' Omar laughed at my outrage.

I know we British are accused of being sentimental about animals in a way few other nations are, but it seemed unnatural to me to eat elephants and I said so.

'Oh, no, we've got to protect the elephants!' Omar adopted a high-pitched, prissy voice, supposedly an imitation of mine. 'If people need to eat, they should eat.' He seemed to think my attitude was middle-class and imperialist and totally out of touch with the poor of the world, which enraged me, as I am proud of my left-wing credentials.

Of course, it turned out that the steaks weren't elephant meat at all; they were extra-large beef steaks. Nevertheless it highlighted a difference in our backgrounds, and I think it's quite funny now that one of our first big arguments was about elephant steaks.

The Cuban Boys were playing New Year's Eve at the club in Kuala Lumpur, then on New Year's Day 1996 the club closed, a month short of the end of their contract. Because of visa problems, they had to stay in Asia until their next contract began on 1 February, so I found a short-term contract for them at a new branch of the Hard Rock Café in Manila. They were to fly to the Philippines on New Year's Day, where I would join them later. I already knew how difficult it can be for Cubans to travel – they need visas to go to the toilet – but I was unprepared for the fact that as soon as they reached passport control at Manila Airport they would be arrested and led away at gunpoint.

Omar had made enquiries at the Philippine Embassy in Kuala Lumpur and had been told they didn't need visas. 'I'm sure you will do,' I'd warned, but he'd brushed it aside. I mentioned it to a friend of ours at the South African Embassy and he was also pretty sure they would need visas, but he phoned the Philippine Embassy and they confirmed that no visas were needed since the band had work permits. Unfortunately this wasn't true and they were arrested as soon as they arrived.

I phoned one of our friends at the South African Consulate to ask for help and he pulled out all the stops to fix things, but it was New Year's Day and everyone was on holiday, so it took a while. Meanwhile I heard that some of the boys in the band were getting bored, tossing rubbish in the wastepaper bin but looking clandestine about it. The guards were holding AK47s, so it seemed unbelievably stupid to me. Eventually it was sorted out and they were free to enter the country and play, but I was beginning to realise that from then on I needed to manage all the band's practical arrangements, including visas. Having a British passport and speaking English as my mother tongue made it so much easier for me than it was for them.

'Good idea,' said Omar with a shrug when I suggested it. 'Why not?'

Omar's birthday is 20 January and I wanted to give him a very special surprise as it was the first of his birthdays on which we'd been together. I was due to receive a chunk of money for an article I'd written and I decided I wanted to buy him an electric violin I knew he admired, a Zeta. It cost over £1,000, but my fee for the article would cover that. I looked but couldn't find a Zeta in Manila. We'd seen one in Singapore, but I hadn't had any money then. The money came through on the 18th, so I had to get one flown over from Singapore if I could find a way to pay for it. I needed it on the 19th, so I could give it to Omar as the clock struck midnight.

An English girl who worked at the Hard Rock Café in Manila agreed to put the cost on her credit card if I gave her the cash. We called the store in Singapore and they took her details and said they would put the violin on the next plane – they did, but the plane was going to Japan. Many frantic calls later, it got back to Manila on the 19th just before 5 p.m. The officials told me I would have it the next day. It wouldn't be there for midnight and I began to get upset. All my plans!

Luckily, another band was playing at the same venue as the Cuban Boys and their leader, Bani, was from Singapore and used to making things move, so he offered them US$50 to clear it and get it in a delivery van to us. Thank heavens for people who know what they're doing.

It was an effort trying to keep Omar out of the way that evening when the parcel was being delivered. I didn't want him to see it because I knew it would probably say 'Zeta' on the packaging. We'd had an argument earlier and Omar kept trying to make it up with me, but I had to pretend I was still angry and not speaking to him to keep him out of the way.

When the parcel arrived, Jas, the singer in Bani's group, and I sneaked it upstairs, opened it and found they'd sent the wrong violin. It was black and Omar wanted a white Zeta. It was also the wrong shape. Beggars can't be choosers, though. It was cheaper than it should have been because they couldn't sell this one.

Bani's band were scheduled to be on stage at midnight, so he and I arranged a way of presenting my gift to Omar. It went according to plan. At midnight Bani asked Omar up to play a number with them, but after a few bars he stopped him.

'That doesn't sound right,' he said. 'Maybe it's because we all have electric pianos and electric guitars, while you're on acoustic violin. Perhaps you could try playing this,' and he pulled out the Zeta and handed it over.

Omar stared at it in shock. He looked at me, and he looked over at the Cuban Boys, who were cheering in the wings. Then he took the violin and started playing. Bani had tuned it and the sound was amazing. Usually Omar's very protective of his acoustic violin – it belonged to his dad and had helped him pay his way through medical school – but when he left the stage that night he actually left it behind. I have never seen him so shocked, before or since.

It turned out that the Zeta they sent was midi-compatible, meaning Omar could use it with a synthesiser. He still cherished his father's violin, but this beautiful, sleek violin was special too, and had proved to be full of surprises. It has always been affectionately known by Omar as 'My Missus'.

I used to get very tired in Manila because it was a humid time of year, but I pushed myself to keep going. Just outside our hotel there was an overpass across a busy road. You had to walk up some steps, along the top, then down the other side. There was a 7-Eleven just the other side. One evening I decided to buy some beers for the boys, so I challenged myself to manage it alone. I got across, bought the beers, made it all the way back, then collapsed up in our room, but I felt more proud than if I had climbed a mountain. It was the same buzz as the first time I jumped out of an aeroplane. I was only walking across an urban overpass, but it was a huge adventure and I felt such a sense of achievement afterwards.

When the contract in Manila came to an end we all went back to Singapore for a new three-month contract at the Coco Carib, a popular club situated on Boat Quay by the riverside. It was great to get back to the city and catch up with all our friends there, but I could feel I was weaker than when we had lived there the previous year. I picked up some writing work, but I wasn't strong enough to go on Adventure Travel trips for Peter any more. There were a few nasty falls when my legs collapsed under me and I cut myself trying to break my fall. I'd also started to suffer from annoying spasms that made my back arch and my legs twitch. I hated this new sign that all wasn't well in my nervous system. I didn't have the energy to go out to clubs late at night, and the daytime heat bothered me, but I could still meet friends in air-conditioned cafés and bars, and I did my best to carry on as before.

As well as the deterioration in my walking, further horrible symptoms were making an appearance. For some time my bladder muscles had been getting weaker, so I'd learned not to drink too much unless I was going to be near a toilet. I would be diving for the loo after downing even one small glass of water. However, my bladder wasn't contracting properly, so I never managed to empty it completely and I started getting urinary-tract infections, which were annoying, and which meant I had to take frequent courses of antibiotics. Then something happened that felt like the worst thing in the world: bowel incontinence.

I was in a hotel, walking across the lobby on my way to interview someone, when my bowels just opened. I rushed straight to the public toilet and locked myself in a cubicle, wishing the ground would open up and swallow me. I'd had moments before when I felt as though I was going to have an involuntary bowel movement, but I'd been able to stop it by sitting down and concentrating hard on tensing the muscles. This time, though, there had been no warning.

I cleaned myself up as best I could, then got a taxi back to the house, where I threw all my clothes straight in the washing machine. I had to phone and say I wasn't well enough to do the interview. I took a shower and wandered around the house in a towel, crying uncontrollably. No one else was at home that day, so I hung up my laundry to dry and sat down to cry some more. If I couldn't control my bowels, that was it – I couldn't go out of the house any more. I'd be like an old lady in a nursing home, with ancillaries coming to change my incontinence pads every few hours. I would stink. I wouldn't be able to have sex any more. Omar wouldn't fancy me now – how could he? Surely this would be the final straw and he'd leave me. Why would he want to be with someone who could hardly walk and was liable to have an embarrassing accident at any moment?

I knew the band was out for dinner and I needed to talk to someone, so I walked up there, still crying my eyes out. As soon as he saw me, Omar took me into a corner, poured me a glass of red wine and said, 'Debbie, what's the problem?'

Although his English was improving, I had to explain to him what had happened in stilted baby language. When he finally understood, to my complete chagrin he burst into fits of laughter.

'Shut up! Why are you laughing? That's mean.'

His laugh was so infectious that I found the corners of my mouth turning up, despite myself.

At last he controlled himself enough to talk. 'OK, OK. Do you want me to cry with you, or do you want me to laugh at you? It's up to you.'

I looked into his compassionate brown eyes and decided that I would much rather we could laugh about things. I was grateful to him for not making a big deal of it. He soon showed me that it didn't change anything for him. He still fancied me and he still wanted to make love to me, and that was more important than ever as far as I was concerned.

After the Singapore contract ended in April 1996, I didn't have anything else lined up until the Montreux Jazz Festival came round again in July. The band didn't have the money to keep flying back to Cuba between jobs, but they couldn't get tourist visas to stay anywhere in the Far East. Being Cuban, they could only get into a country if they had the correct visa and they only got that with a work contract, so they were in a bind. I asked around and finally managed to get them a six-week booking on a cruise ship sailing between Singapore, Kuala Lumpur and the Thai resort of Phuket.

It was lovely at first, but before long the band was calling the ship their 'golden prison'. With a British passport I could get off and go exploring whenever we stopped in a port, but they had to stay on board.

'At least you're not cleaning the toilets,' I told them. An English band that was also on board had been signed on as crew, which meant that when they weren't playing they had to muck in and help look after the paying guests. I had made sure that the Cuban Boys were signed on as artistes, so they avoided that fate.

By the time we reached Phuket the band had severe cabin fever, so I consulted the captain. He said that Thailand was the only place on the cruise where he could bribe the port authorities to let them ashore for a day, so that's what he did. We were sailing between the three ports, so every time we reached Phuket the band members were able to go to the beach for a change of scene.

I was increasingly fatigued during this trip, but when I looked at the visible poverty throughout that part of the world I felt I had no right to complain. In Manila I had heard that many poor people give their children to orphanages because it is the only way they can get enough food to eat and a rudimentary education. I visited an orphanage there and found the rows and rows of cots utterly depressing. Even that was better than the sights I saw in Phuket, though, where starving children with visible ribs sat on street corners begging. They suffered from all kinds of horrific diseases that we have cures for in the West – rickets, scurvy and leprosy, for example. There were kids who'd lost limbs and who, instead of having a nice wheelchair to get around in, sat in upturned crates attached to bicycle wheels and propelled themselves along.

Even worse, I walked through the back streets of Phuket and saw young girls, much younger than 16, offering themselves to middle-aged male tourists. They had huge dark eyes, lips smeared with lipstick and skinny little prepubescent bodies. The sight of them selling themselves made me feel sick and enraged, but there was nothing I could do. I felt horrible guilt at the differences between us. I wasn't rich by Western standards, but I had credit cards and access to the kind of money that would buy me food and a decent roof over my head wherever I went. I could sell an article, while those girls had nothing to sell but themselves. I don't know how much they were making in their sordid transactions with white men, but I bet it wasn't much more than the price of a bag of rice.

Like me, Omar was horrified by what he saw. He said that nothing like that could happen in Cuba, where there is no homelessness and everyone gets food, healthcare and education. Of course every country in the world has prostitutes, but the Thai ones were unbelievably young and were doing it simply so that they and their families could stay alive, and that upset us a lot. No matter what happened to me, I was lucky compared to them, and that was a lesson worth learning.

Nevertheless, in my head I was starting to realise that my time in the Far East was running out. Back in Brighton my doctor had mentioned that a hot climate can make MS symptoms worse. Did that mean that if I went home to the UK they would get better? I didn't have a doctor in the Far East who could offer advice, but I knew I was getting to the stage where I was going to need medical help close at hand.

One thing stopped me: if I went back to Britain, what would happen to my relationship with Omar? I couldn't expect him to come and stay with me for long, because he was a member of a band based in Cuba that earned a living touring the Far East. I didn't even know if he'd be able to get a visa to visit me in Britain. Would that be difficult? I was about to find out.

Chapter 7

'Your Grass Is White'

'I need to go home, Omar. I need to be closer to my doctor.'

'Uh-huh.'

'Will you come and visit me sometimes? When you're flying back to Cuba and have a European stopover maybe.'

'Well, I never thought of visiting England before, but if you are there, of course I will.'

'I thought I would go back right after New Year.' The band was flying back to Cuba via Paris; they didn't need visas because they would only be in the airport. The stop was about three hours, just long enough to change planes. I asked him if it was possible to change the flight. Would he like to visit the UK?

'Why not?'

We applied for a tourist visa for him while we were in Singapore, but before it came through we had to fly back to Kuala Lumpur, where the band was booked to play from October through to New Year's Eve. The gig was at a hotel and we were given rooms there, which was good because it meant there was no housework to do.

I was using two walking sticks to keep my balance as I went around town, and I called taxis whenever I had any distance to cover, but I was shocked by what one taxi driver said to me.

'People like you shouldn't go out.'

'Pardon?'

'You just make things difficult for everyone else by slowing them up and getting in the way.'

I was speechless. I'd wondered if I might be discriminated against because of my MS, but I'd never encountered anything except helpfulness in Singapore, Manila and all the other places I'd visited with the band. Maybe taxi drivers in Kuala Lumpur have attitude, though, because Omar had a run-in with one who insisted that Fidel Castro was the devil incarnate.

It's not as if all disabilities were covered up in Kuala Lumpur – quite the opposite. We came upon a branch of Kentucky Fried Chicken that was staffed entirely by deaf people. You had to point at what you wanted on the menu. I thought it was refreshing to recognise what people can do, rather than concentrate on what they can't. We would go out of our way to take our custom there, and I don't think we were alone.

Our visa application was transferred across to the British Embassy in Kuala Lumpur and Omar and I were invited in to be interviewed separately. I faced a barrage of questions about our relationship, the gist of which was, 'Are you a genuine couple?' I wondered how we were expected to prove it, short of getting down and having sex on the floor in front of them.

At the end of the interviews I could tell they were still umming and ahing about us. The main problem was that you're not supposed to apply for a tourist visa from a third country. I wondered if I should have brought my wheelchair along and gone for the sympathy vote, but it had been too complicated to get it there.

The day after our interviews at the embassy we went to see some Colombian friends of ours playing a gig. By this stage I couldn't dance any more. My body just didn't respond the way I wanted it to and I felt too unstable. Nevertheless that night Omar swept me on to the floor, pulled me close, then lifted me up to stand on his feet as he whirled me round the room, the way uncles do with their little nieces at weddings. It was a lovely evening.

Just as we were leaving, a man came over to us and I recognised him as one of the officials from the British Embassy.

'Did you have a good evening?' he asked, smiling.

'Yes, thanks.'

'I'm not supposed to tell you this, but it's so obvious you two are a real couple that I'll make sure the visa you want is ready on Monday.'

He winked at us and disappeared before I could even thank him.

I went to the embassy on Monday morning (or what passes for the morning when you live with musicians) and there was the visa, just as he'd promised. The first hurdle was out of the way: Omar could come to Bradford. But would he like it? If only he wasn't coming for the first time in January. It was the worst possible month of the year for him to form an impression of our 'green and pleasant land', because it would undoubtedly be grey and miserable, cold and raining. I'd just have to do my best to make it fun, regardless of the weather.

I was flying back a week before him, landing at Gatwick and transferring to Leeds by train. My brother offered to meet me at the airport and drive me across town to King's Cross Station, but there was a direct train and I didn't want him to have to take the time off work, so I declined. I hadn't reckoned on the fact that my legs were stiff and unresponsive after the ten-hour overnight flight from Malaysia. When I landed at Gatwick and found I couldn't walk I still thought there wasn't a problem because I could propel myself along in my wheelchair with my holdall on my knee.

This worked fine at Gatwick, where they had the kind of train that I could roll straight on to without help. Half an hour later I rolled out on to the platform at King's Cross Thameslink. The train continued out of the station, the other passengers disappeared, and I looked around for the lift to street level, but there wasn't one. Where was the disabled access? This was 1997, so surely there was something?

I wheeled myself along the platform and finally found a call button set in the wall. I pressed it and waited. Then I pressed it again. Nothing happened. There was no one in sight. I wheeled myself to the foot of the flight of steps and tried to get up, but my legs weren't working at all, and even if I could have dragged myself up by clinging on to the banister I would still need to get my holdall and wheelchair up somehow. I wheeled myself back to the call button and pressed it again, then burst into tears.

It was horrible feeling utterly helpless and trapped. There was literally nothing I could do. Rationally I knew that someone would come by before too long and I'd be able to summon help, but the feeling of being dependent on strangers was awful. Was this what the future held as my MS progressed? Would this happen to me again and again? I sat on that platform and sobbed my heart out.

I heard another train coming in. The doors opened and passengers alighted.

'Are you all right?' a voice asked. I looked up to see a guy with a really kind face who appeared from his clothing to be a builder of some sort.

'No,' I said through my tears. 'I can't get up the stairs.'

He turned to the passengers making their way down the platform. 'Here, lads, can you give the lady a hand?'

Two men stopped, a besuited businessman and a scruffy student. The businessman nodded, and the student said, 'Sure. No problem.'

The builder and the businessman clasped their hands together to form a sling in which I could sit and they carried me up the stairs, while the student followed with my wheelchair and holdall.

'You sure you're all right now?' the builder asked at the top. 'Which way are you going?'

They put me down in my chair and I sat for a moment at the top of the stairs to compose myself and settle my nerves, still shaken about having to accept help from strangers. When I moved out of the station, I could see my knights standing on the corner exchanging business cards and numbers. They felt somehow connected after their joint achievement in getting me up the stairs. I was pleased to realise that not only are people willing to help a damsel in distress, but they also feel good about themselves when they are able to.

I arrived back in Bradford and had a week to sort things out at my house before Omar came. There had been students living there to keep the house occupied, so it needed a good clean and to be made into my home again. What's more, for the last couple of months it had been empty and a toilet over-flow had dripped down into the kitchen, blowing the electrics. The carpets had to be taken up and the electrics fixed, but fortunately our street is full of talented tradesmen who also happen to be some of the nicest people around.

I was worried that Omar wouldn't like it in England and my anxieties increased further when it started to snow. What would someone who was used to tropical temperatures make of that?

'Your grass is white here,' he said, grinning, when I met him at Heathrow Airport on 15 January 1997. 'What's that about?'

'Haven't you ever seen snow before?'

'Yeah, of course. When I played in Helsinki.' He told me that he'd had holes in the soles of his shoes so had put news-paper inside, but that had proved useless for walking in the snow. Several of the band had the same problem, so they'd ended up having to share shoes on that trip and could never all go out at the same time.

'How was the flight?'

'You English! I got fed up with all the "Please, please, please, thank you, thank you, thank you, sorry, sorry, sorry"!' he said, mimicking our English politeness. 'For God's sake, just give me the water!'

We transferred to a flight up to Leeds, where my neighbour Trisha had volunteered to meet us at the airport. As soon as we stepped out of the terminal, Omar huddled inside his jacket, shocked at the icy temperature.

'Oh, man, how do you people live in this? There's smoke coming out of my mouth. What am I doing here? You have to be crazy.'

When we got back to the house, he couldn't believe that it was even cold inside and he sat shivering in front of the little single electric heater in the sitting room. He soon found that the climate causes major cultural differences as well. In Cuba everyone has their windows open and they spend a lot of time outside in their yards or in the street, chatting to friends and neighbours. In England, with the cold, rain and snow, sometimes the only people you see are those you have actually invited into your home, so it's much less sociable. We shut our doors, draw the curtains and live inside our own four walls, which can feel suffocating to a gregarious Cuban.

Soon after he arrived, I took Omar to the Casa Latina, an underground club in Leeds, where I was friendly with the promoter, Lubie. They had live music, a group of English guys playing Brazilian music, and Omar was introduced to them.

'What do you play?' the band leader asked.

'Violin,' Omar replied, and they looked at him quizzically. It was still seen as a classical instrument in the UK back in 1997, so I expect they wondered what he was doing clutching an electric violin in a Latin club.

'Why don't you ask if you can play a couple of numbers with them?' I suggested.

'They didn't invite me.'

'Just go and show them what you can do with a violin.'

As he made his way to the stage, I wished him luck: 'Kill 'em, cowboy!'

He played a couple of numbers and the buzz was amazing. The crowd really responded to him and there was renewed vigour in everyone's playing as they rose to the challenge of accommodating a new instrument.

After the set Lubie introduced us to Sam, the leader of the Cuban-influenced house band Casa Latina All-Stars. Sam had obviously liked Omar's playing because he suggested he should come and rehearse with the All-Stars, and if they were able to work together, then Sam would apply for a work permit on Omar's behalf.

A few days later, when Omar went to sit in with the All-Stars, he asked me, 'Could you say that thing about the cowboy again?'

'What? Go kill 'em, cowboy?'

'That's it.' He grinned.

From then on it became a ritual before he went on stage anywhere that I had to say, 'Go kill 'em, cowboy!' If I wasn't physically there, I had to call and say it down the phone. A footballer might put on their lucky pants before a match, actors might avoid peacock feathers and tell each other to 'break a leg', but Omar needed me to say, 'Go kill 'em, cowboy!' and I was happy to oblige.

The try-out went well, but afterwards he complained to me about the way English people dance: 'They don't seem to like holding one another.'

Latin people hold each other and move together when they dance, whereas English people only seemed to do that for the slow dance at the end of the evening. Over the next few years, as salsa dancing became more part of British nightlife, Omar began to lighten up on us.

He only spent a month in Bradford on that occasion before he had to go back to Cuba. His flight was departing early in the morning from Gatwick, so the day before we went to a Cuba Solidarity event in London, where we were surprised to meet a dancer called Rodolfo whom Omar had known years before in Havana. His wife, Maria, was an amazing woman who taught wheelchair users to dance, and both were on scholarships at the Laban Institute in London. It seemed like a good omen that Omar had his own friends in England already.

Omar had said he wanted to get back to Bradford as soon as possible to see me, but I knew he wouldn't want to leave the Cuban Boys in the lurch, so I came up with an idea that the whole band could come to Britain and I'd arrange little tours for them. The money would be better than they'd been getting in the Far East and they wouldn't have to play six nights a week. The problem with my plan became obvious, though, as they wouldn't have to work six nights a week because nowhere could sustain that, and if they weren't working, accommodation and food would have to be paid for. Jean-Luc, the ex-manager based in Switzerland, came up with some possible gigs for them in Spain that sounded more suitable, so the rest of the band took the work in Spain, while Omar came to England to be with me. Despite the cold, and the huge cultural differences, he felt his future lay with me. I must say I was very relieved, as I missed him when he wasn't there. Things were easier, and much happier, for me with him around.

He flew back to Bradford in March, and while it was still very chilly by Cuban standards, the skies were blue and the spring flowers were starting to bloom. His application for a six-month work permit, on the grounds that he was a musician with an international reputation, bringing unique skills to the UK, was supposed to be dealt with while he was out of the country, but the Department for Work and Pensions allowed him to return in March as long as he left again when the visa was issued. To my delight, it was granted in May, but visas can't be issued when you are in the country; you need to get them from an overseas embassy and the only country in Europe to which he could travel without a visa was Switzerland. Omar had already spent time working out there and knew that Switzerland was expensive and that we'd never be able to afford to eat, let alone stay, so we went to Asda and bought some yoghurts, made sandwiches and flew to Geneva for a picnic! We spent the night with a Cuban friend of Omar's, went to the British Embassy the next morning and got his passport stamped before flying home again.

We were so broke that Omar offered to apply for unskilled jobs, like a counter assistant in McDonald's or working on a building site. I didn't want him to do that, though, because that's not the man I fell in love with. If I'd fallen in love with a McDonald's assistant, fine, but I didn't. Building sites would be too dangerous for a violinist's hands. I fell in love with a musician and I wanted him to continue to focus on his music, so we agreed that's what he would do, even if we were poor as church mice in the meantime.

Through friends we met a Cuban timbales player called Félix, and one night when he and I were chatting we came up with the idea to form an informal cooperative of Cuban musicians who were living in the UK, which would help them to find their feet and get work. We could call it Raíces Cubanas, which means 'Cuban Roots', and Omar could be the band leader.

At first Omar said, 'Forget it!' He enjoyed playing but was fed up with being a band leader, even with me helping with the business side of things. He couldn't shrug off responsibility, which could be heavy. Besides, he wanted to work on his own compositions. Finally I persuaded him it could be a loose collective that wouldn't be too much responsibility and I volunteered to do the administration. We put together a band of five or six guys who were flexible about the instruments they played depending on who was available on the night, so that Omar could sometimes find himself on bass, piano, or even singing. We had to use a Colombian percussionist because we couldn't find a Cuban one. (How times change.) It took a bit of rehearsal and a lot of patience to get them organised, but they sounded great and they felt good earning some money and having more control.

While Omar was beginning to establish himself in the UK, I was going for appointments with my new neurologist, Mark Busby, at St Luke's Hospital in Bradford. Right from the start I had total respect for him. He was a no-nonsense type of man (and good-looking), which was exactly what I wanted (the attitude, not the looks). I felt he listened to me as well. After our first meeting, he ran through a list of alternative therapies.

'Some people think reflexology helps, or acupuncture, homeopathy, hyperbaric treatments – you'll find all kinds of suggestions on the internet. As a scientist I think they're not effective, but some people with MS swear they work, and if any of them work for you I won't tell you not to use them.'

I had heard things about all of these alternative treatments from friends and had read about them on the internet, and had been geared up to do battle with Dr Busby in order to discuss them. He totally disarmed me. I hadn't expected a neurologist to be so open. I think candid discussion about these things is essential to good communication about MS.

A friend in Norway had used hyperbaric treatment and swore it helped MS, so I booked an appointment when I visited. I was put inside a pressurised chamber, like a diving bell, and the air pressure was increased. The theory is that oxygen is transported more efficiently in the blood cells at higher pressure. These tanks are used to treat divers with decompression sickness and people with carbon-monoxide poisoning. There is some evidence that they could improve motor skills (in other words the ability to move!) in people with multiple sclerosis. At the end of the treatment you are gradually brought back to normal air pressure so that you don't get the bends.

I'd heard that a lot of MS patients rave about the benefits of hyperbaric treatment, so I walked out of the chamber scrutinising the way my legs were moving and wondering if there was any difference. When I woke the next morning I swung my legs round and raised myself up from the bed, so optimistic that I was going to feel a change that for a short while I managed to convince myself that maybe I was balancing slightly better than normal, and maybe I was walking down the stairs more steadily. In actual fact, though, I don't think it made any difference at all. I'm sure it does for some people, just not for me.

My cousin Kim recommended that I ate a macrobiotic diet. I read up about it and found you are allowed grains, pulses, vegetables, fruit and seaweed, but you have to balance each meal between so-called yin and yang elements. You're not allowed meat, wheat, cheese, chocolate, wine, tea or processed foods. A typical meal would be something like sautéed butternut squash, leek and cabbage with brown rice.

I thought about it, but it wasn't really me, and Omar wouldn't touch it.

'What is this bloody stuff? Are you trying to turn me into a rabbit like you?'

I did a bit of reflexology, which was basically a nice foot massage, and read up about goat serum, another of the treatments I'd heard of. It was still being trialled for use on MS. I also read about a woman called Cari Loder who had pioneered her own MS treatment combining an antidepressant, an amino acid found in diet cola and vitamin B12. She'd written a book about her findings called *Standing in the Sunshine*, and a big drugs company was paying to put it through pharmaceutical trials. I thought there must be something in it, but decided to wait and see how the trials went.

There seemed to be a million different people out there advocating complex regimes and substances you had to buy. Everyone thought they had found the answer. After trying a few fads of the moment, I decided I didn't want to have my hopes raised and dashed time after time. I was finding out that some people with MS try every new drug and treatment in the hope of either a cure or at least alleviation of their symptoms, and that is great for them, but I couldn't handle the emotional rollercoaster each time I tried something new and saw no difference at all. I'd rather get on with my life and put my trust in the NHS. If there was a cure, they'd soon yell at me about it!

Mark Busby's apparent open mind was incredibly refreshing. By mentioning alternative therapies but not encouraging me to explore them, he let me come to my own conclusions. For that I am eternally grateful, as I think it helped me to accept responsibility for dealing with my MS.

I decided to teach Omar to drive because he needed to be able to get to gigs without me and without spending his entire earnings on transport. I was becoming less confident about driving as my legs got weaker and it was good to have someone to take over. So we set out one brisk April morning in my little Ford Escort, a nightmare of a car with an oil leak that meant I had to carry a spare can around wherever I went. The driver's side window wouldn't stay up unless I jammed in a piece of folded paper, but it had only cost £200, so I couldn't complain. Omar later wrote a song about it called 'Mi Carro'.

By the time we reached the end of the road that first day, I had already screeched in panic at his gung-ho approach to driving. It was a terrifying experience and a huge test of our relationship. I've taught a number of people to drive and never had a problem with it, but I say to anyone now, never teach your partner to drive, especially if they're a man! I kept telling myself that if we got through this without killing each other, we'd be stronger as a couple.

We were coming back from visiting friends near Penrith one day, travelling along narrow, winding roads. There were double white lines in the middle of the road and we were approaching a humpback bridge when Omar suddenly decided to overtake a tractor with huge bundles of hay on its trailer.

'Stop! Brake! Pull in!' I yelled, but Omar thought it was just because I didn't want to teach him about overtaking.

'Chill out, Debbie,' he said, ignoring me.

We got past without incident, but I screamed at him, 'You idiot!' Actually, I wasn't that polite, but I'm pretty sure if I tried to write my words there would only be a row of asterisks.

'You are too tense,' he told me calmly, and we continued on our way.

Omar's idea of lightening the mood when we have an argument in the car is to put his foot down on the brake and come to a stop right in the middle of the road. This was the first time I ever experienced this.

'Tell me you love me,' he demanded.

'Omar, for God's sake, keep driving,' I snapped. Another driver was waiting behind us with growing impatience, trying to figure out what we were doing.

'Tell me you love me.'

'Start the bloody car.'

'Tell me you love me.'

'For God's sake, start the car.'

'Tell me you love me.'

'OK, OK, I love you.'

At last he released the handbrake and moved on. There are times in an argument with Omar when the only sensible course is to let him have his way.

If you don't speak English as a first language, you can pay to take the written part of the driving test using a translator, but we couldn't afford that. Instead he spent two weeks memorising the Highway Code from start to finish. There is that to happen. It would make it easier for Omar to find work in the UK once he had residency and then hopefully we'd have more money. All my friends liked him – in fact, lots of my friends seemed to think he was nicer than me.

Before it could happen, though, he would have to go back to Cuba to get divorced. I decided I wanted to go along. I was keen to see his homeland, meet his mother and nephews, and get more of a sense of the environment in which he had grown up. If we went early enough in the year, it shouldn't be too hot for me and we could stay with his mum in the apartment near the Malecón.

As soon as we drove into Havana I fell in love with it. The whole place was beautiful. It had a kind of decaying decadence, with ornate buildings lining streets full of 1950s classic cars – Chevys and Cadillacs – all dilapidated but somehow still running. There's beautiful coloured tiling on the building fronts and in the lobbies, and everywhere the sound of music floats out of open windows or drifts up from the Malecón. It's a city full of music, where everyone seems to play or sing or dance.

Omar's mother, Gloria, was like a short female version of Omar. She had a similarly upbeat personality and the same naughty eyes and pronounced cheekbones. She used to work as a midwife and she loved children – especially Omar, who was her baby. She was beaming from ear to ear as we walked up the steps to the flat, and could hardly bring herself to stop hugging him for the first hour we were there. I could tell right away he was a mummy's boy from the secret grins they shared and the way Gloria fussed around him, making

a book containing the 635 possible driving-test questions and he learned every single question and answer off by heart. When he sat the test he got 100 per cent in the written exam. Seeing how much Omar's driving improved after his theory test, I think the government should consider making people pass their theory test before they are allowed on the road at all.

Once Omar could drive, he did. I wasn't managing to do any work, so we were dependent on my incapacity benefit and whatever he could earn playing with the Casa Latina All-Stars and Raíces Cubanas. I'd been working less and less even before my diagnosis because I couldn't commit to copy deadlines any more, or do the kind of marketing jobs I had experience in. Some days I was fine, but on other days I was too tired to work, and it wasn't fair to let people down.

I considered doing a bit of freelance journalism, but I didn't have the contacts in Bradford and I had no qualifications and couldn't really drive any more. I suppose I could have sent out emails introducing myself, but my dexterity was failing, my mobility was restrictive, and I didn't want to put myself under any unnecessary pressure. There were mornings when it took all my energy just to get up and dressed; sometimes I stayed in bed, too exhausted to do more than stagger to the toilet.

But then something happened that put it all into context. At the end of 1997 my big sister Tina had a stroke and was initially paralysed by it. Omar and I drove to visit her at the Queen's Medical Centre in Nottingham and I was desperately upset to see her lying there. Her speech was so slurred you could barely make out the words, and the left side of her face was collapsed into the pillow. Everyone else on the stroke ward was elderly apart from her. Now that really wasn't fair. Omar got his violin from the car and wandered up and down the ward giving everyone an impromptu concert, while I sat and held Tina's hand and tried to understand what she was saying.

I'd been closest to Tina when I was young, despite the nine-year age gap between us. She used to babysit for me when she was a teenager, and it provided a handy alibi when she wanted to date a boyfriend. The boyfriends paid for me to have ice-skating lessons at the rink, or swimming lessons in the local pool, so that she could spend some time with them while I learned a new skill. I thought my big sister was impossibly glamorous when she got all dressed up, with her jewellery and styled hair. I went through a phase when I wanted to grow up to be exactly like her.

Now she was lying in bed, helpless. I wiped a trail of saliva from the corner of her mouth and kissed her forehead. The unpredictable, catastrophic nature of stroke seemed much worse to me than MS. My symptoms developed gradually and I had time to work out how to deal with them, but she had been struck down without warning, leaving her husband and two children at home to manage without her.

Luckily, she mostly recovered over the next few weeks and regained a semblance of normality, but it was a wake-up call for me. I had to be grateful for what I had. Wherever I went, there were always going to be people worse off than me.

Chapter 8

In Sickness and in Health

In November 1997 I received a marriage proposal – not from Omar, but from a man called Adrian at the Department for Work and Pensions. Omar's six-month work permit w running out and we had applied to extend it for another months, on the same basis as before – that he was a musi with an international reputation and brought a weal experience to the British music scene.

I asked how we could get his residence status on to permanent footing and Adrian said, 'I can't keep e the work permits. Why don't you two get married?

Omar and I looked at each other. I'd never see the marrying kind and he was still married to Ja

'We'll think about it,' I said.

And when we thought about it, we realised Omar said, 'Why not? We're adults. We like e let's get married.'

We'd been together for three years, w together, and this was the best way to get sure he was comfortable, bringing drinks and snacks and adjusting the cushions.

The flat had been split into two because Gloria used to live in one side and Omar and Jamilla in the other. Omar told me it had been a volatile arrangement at times, as his wife and his mother were both strong women. I can imagine Gloria felt that no one was good enough for her precious son. There would probably have been explosions if I lived there long term, but since she spoke very little English and we were just there for a month, problems didn't arise on my visit.

I was supposed to meet Jamilla during that trip, but she couldn't get back from Italy, so it didn't happen. I know she must be a nice woman for Omar to have married her in the first place. I couldn't imagine him going out with anyone I wouldn't like. While we were in Havana, Omar organised the divorce papers and sent them over to her and she signed them and sent them back. It was all totally amicable. I spoke to her on the phone a few times and I thought she sounded lovely.

Omar's two youngest nephews, Aaron and Ramses, were teenagers at the time we went out and it was obvious how much they looked up to their dad's baby brother. They were both studying music: Aaron plays bass, and Ramses violin. Omar's other nephew, Victor, came up from Santiago, bringing his baby son, who was just starting to toddle, and Uncle Omar had a great time with them all. He was (and is) very proud of them.

We spent our days walking the streets of Old Havana, eating food bought from street vendors – paper cones of peanuts or fruit sorbets sold out of the front windows of people's homes – looking at sights like the atmospheric Museum of the Revolution and the Governor General's Palace. In the evening we went out to bars like El Floridita, where Hemingway used to drink his daiquiris, and La Bodeguita, where he drank his mojitos. I was introduced to lots of Omar's friends. Some were playing in the places we went. They visited us or we visited them – it didn't matter but it was always raucous and loud.

There was music everywhere we went and I could see how Omar must have been steeped in it as he grew up, and how his tastes must have been shaped by just living in such a vibrant city: we heard salsa, merengue, jazz, *son* and classical music wherever we went. Havana has a distinctive rhythm. Omar did some teaching at the Escuela Nacional de Arte while we were there, not to earn money: these institutions don't have much, and now that he was working overseas he was solvent (though still pretty broke by Western standards). He regularly sent money back to his family in Havana, even when we were skint and unable to meet the mortgage payment.

The American trade embargo causes real harm to Cuba, because no country so tiny can possibly make everything it needs, and there are shortages of vital medicines and agricultural products. Even fruits and vegetables are in short supply, so Cuba, with its 'get on with it' attitude, turned beautiful flowerbeds into vegetable patches. I think that's the way Omar copes with my MS: if you can't change it, you may as well make the best of it. Cuba doesn't present a threat to the US, a book containing the 635 possible driving-test questions and he learned every single question and answer off by heart. When he sat the test he got 100 per cent in the written exam. Seeing how much Omar's driving improved after his theory test, I think the government should consider making people pass their theory test before they are allowed on the road at all.

Once Omar could drive, he did. I wasn't managing to do any work, so we were dependent on my incapacity benefit and whatever he could earn playing with the Casa Latina All-Stars and Raíces Cubanas. I'd been working less and less even before my diagnosis because I couldn't commit to copy deadlines any more, or do the kind of marketing jobs I had experience in. Some days I was fine, but on other days I was too tired to work, and it wasn't fair to let people down.

I considered doing a bit of freelance journalism, but I didn't have the contacts in Bradford and I had no qualifications and couldn't really drive any more. I suppose I could have sent out emails introducing myself, but my dexterity was failing, my mobility was restrictive, and I didn't want to put myself under any unnecessary pressure. There were mornings when it took all my energy just to get up and dressed; sometimes I stayed in bed, too exhausted to do more than stagger to the toilet.

But then something happened that put it all into context. At the end of 1997 my big sister Tina had a stroke and was initially paralysed by it. Omar and I drove to visit her at the Queen's Medical Centre in Nottingham and I was desperately upset to see her lying there. Her speech was so slurred you could barely make out the words, and the left side of her face was collapsed into the pillow. Everyone else on the stroke ward was elderly apart from her. Now that really wasn't fair. Omar got his violin from the car and wandered up and down the ward giving everyone an impromptu concert, while I sat and held Tina's hand and tried to understand what she was saying.

I'd been closest to Tina when I was young, despite the nine-year age gap between us. She used to babysit for me when she was a teenager, and it provided a handy alibi when she wanted to date a boyfriend. The boyfriends paid for me to have ice-skating lessons at the rink, or swimming lessons in the local pool, so that she could spend some time with them while I learned a new skill. I thought my big sister was impossibly glamorous when she got all dressed up, with her jewellery and styled hair. I went through a phase when I wanted to grow up to be exactly like her.

Now she was lying in bed, helpless. I wiped a trail of saliva from the corner of her mouth and kissed her forehead. The unpredictable, catastrophic nature of stroke seemed much worse to me than MS. My symptoms developed gradually and I had time to work out how to deal with them, but she had been struck down without warning, leaving her husband and two children at home to manage without her.

Luckily, she mostly recovered over the next few weeks and regained a semblance of normality, but it was a wake-up call for me. I had to be grateful for what I had. Wherever I went, there were always going to be people worse off than me.

Chapter 8

In Sickness and in Health

In November 1997 I received a marriage proposal – not from Omar, but from a man called Adrian at the Department for Work and Pensions. Omar's six-month work permit was running out and we had applied to extend it for another six months, on the same basis as before – that he was a musician with an international reputation and brought a wealth of experience to the British music scene.

I asked how we could get his residence status on to a more permanent footing and Adrian said, 'I can't keep extending the work permits. Why don't you two get married?'

Omar and I looked at each other. I'd never seen myself as the marrying kind and he was still married to Jamilla.

'We'll think about it,' I said.

And when we thought about it, we realised it made sense. Omar said, 'Why not? We're adults. We like each other. Yeah, let's get married.'

We'd been together for three years, we wanted to stay together, and this was the best way to get legal permission for that to happen. It would make it easier for Omar to find work in the UK once he had residency and then hopefully we'd have more money. All my friends liked him – in fact, lots of my friends seemed to think he was nicer than me.

Before it could happen, though, he would have to go back to Cuba to get divorced. I decided I wanted to go along. I was keen to see his homeland, meet his mother and nephews, and get more of a sense of the environment in which he had grown up. If we went early enough in the year, it shouldn't be too hot for me and we could stay with his mum in the apartment near the Malecón.

As soon as we drove into Havana I fell in love with it. The whole place was beautiful. It had a kind of decaying decadence, with ornate buildings lining streets full of 1950s classic cars – Chevys and Cadillacs – all dilapidated but somehow still running. There's beautiful coloured tiling on the building fronts and in the lobbies, and everywhere the sound of music floats out of open windows or drifts up from the Malecón. It's a city full of music, where everyone seems to play or sing or dance.

Omar's mother, Gloria, was like a short female version of Omar. She had a similarly upbeat personality and the same naughty eyes and pronounced cheekbones. She used to work as a midwife and she loved children – especially Omar, who was her baby. She was beaming from ear to ear as we walked up the steps to the flat, and could hardly bring herself to stop hugging him for the first hour we were there. I could tell straight away he was a mummy's boy from the secret grins they shared and the way Gloria fussed around him, making sure he was comfortable, bringing drinks and snacks and adjusting the cushions.

The flat had been split into two because Gloria used to live in one side and Omar and Jamilla in the other. Omar told me it had been a volatile arrangement at times, as his wife and his mother were both strong women. I can imagine Gloria felt that no one was good enough for her precious son. There would probably have been explosions if I lived there long term, but since she spoke very little English and we were just there for a month, problems didn't arise on my visit.

I was supposed to meet Jamilla during that trip, but she couldn't get back from Italy, so it didn't happen. I know she must be a nice woman for Omar to have married her in the first place. I couldn't imagine him going out with anyone I wouldn't like. While we were in Havana, Omar organised the divorce papers and sent them over to her and she signed them and sent them back. It was all totally amicable. I spoke to her on the phone a few times and I thought she sounded lovely.

Omar's two youngest nephews, Aaron and Ramses, were teenagers at the time we went out and it was obvious how much they looked up to their dad's baby brother. They were both studying music: Aaron plays bass, and Ramses violin. Omar's other nephew, Victor, came up from Santiago, bringing his baby son, who was just starting to toddle, and Uncle Omar had a great time with them all. He was (and is) very proud of them.

We spent our days walking the streets of Old Havana, eating food bought from street vendors – paper cones of peanuts or fruit sorbets sold out of the front windows of people's homes – looking at sights like the atmospheric Museum of the Revolution and the Governor General's Palace. In the evening we went out to bars like El Floridita, where Hemingway used to drink his daiquiris, and La Bodeguita, where he drank his mojitos. I was introduced to lots of Omar's friends. Some were playing in the places we went. They visited us or we visited them – it didn't matter but it was always raucous and loud.

There was music everywhere we went and I could see how Omar must have been steeped in it as he grew up, and how his tastes must have been shaped by just living in such a vibrant city: we heard salsa, merengue, jazz, *son* and classical music wherever we went. Havana has a distinctive rhythm. Omar did some teaching at the Escuela Nacional de Arte while we were there, not to earn money: these institutions don't have much, and now that he was working overseas he was solvent (though still pretty broke by Western standards). He regularly sent money back to his family in Havana, even when we were skint and unable to meet the mortgage payment.

The American trade embargo causes real harm to Cuba, because no country so tiny can possibly make everything it needs, and there are shortages of vital medicines and agricul- tural products. Even fruits and vegetables are in short supply, so Cuba, with its 'get on with it' attitude, turned beautiful flowerbeds into vegetable patches. I think that's the way Omar copes with my MS: if you can't change it, you may as well make the best of it. Cuba doesn't present a threat to the US, as they don't have the money or will to threaten their neighbour after the disintegration of the USSR during the 1980s and early 1990s. There could be no fears that shipments of nuclear missiles might turn up on Cuban shores, so the whole blockade feels outdated and vindictive.

The Cubans research and test their own medicines and have developed some that are more effective than the equivalents used in the West. The meningitis jab we use in the UK was first developed in Cuba. They have become a nation of mechanics, keeping cars running that were brought over in the 1950s and fixing machinery rather than replacing it. They find ingenious solutions to the shortages and live their lives under the shadow of their neighbour with a cheerful resilience. I came away with a massive respect for the Cuban people, and a deeper understanding of Omar's pride in his country.

Gloria wasn't able to come over to Bradford for our wedding, but she gave us her blessing and said she was delighted to welcome me into her family. It must have been hard for her to wave us off at the end of the trip, knowing she would see even less of her precious son now that he was living with me in the UK, but if that upset her she didn't show it. She was warm and loving to me throughout our time there.

On 14 May 1998 Lubie had invited Raíces Cubanas to come and play at the Casa Latina, and because it meant that lots of our friends would be in town anyway Omar and I decided that that was the day we would get married. Our reception could be at the club. It was a win-win situation because we got a wedding party for our friends and, what's more, Omar would be getting paid for being there! So we married at Adrian's suggestion, and Lubie set the date. How romantic!

We didn't have money to pay for a big fancy wedding, and I had no parents to contribute, so I managed to arrange the whole day for the sum total of £110, almost half of which went to the registry office. My wedding outfit was a pair of white trousers with an elasticated waist and a white sleeveless T-shirt from Marks & Spencer. I found it hard to get dressed in anything with buttons and fiddly bits, so pull-on trousers had become my staple look.

My neighbour Trisha made a white wedding cake for us. The weather was fantastic, so strawberries were cheap and we bought loads of punnets for a knock-down price at Asda. We bulk-bought dozens of bottles of beer and a few cheap bottles of wine, and put them in a big black plastic tub. A friend got ice from the local pub to chill them. The lady at our nearest Interflora sold me a bouquet of lilies for next to nothing because they had already opened, and she made buttonholes from yellow roses for the men to wear in their lapels. She delivered several bouquets from friends who hadn't been able to come, and made the bouquets to complement each other and the wedding flowers. It wasn't elaborate, but it was a special day because of the thoughts of family and friends.

Our biggest expenditure, other than the registry office, was the rings: Omar's was £19.99 and mine was £14.99 from one of those places that sell cheap gold. We joked to everyone that it was a buy-one-get-one-free deal. They're actually perfectly nice rings.

I wasn't overly sentimental about the whole event, but I wanted to look my best on the day, so Suzanne helped. She's a beautician and could do the waxing, make-up, hairstyling and fake tan. I was so happy with the final result. Omar, more so. He was delighted to see I could look like a lady. All Omar got out of the day was a new shirt and tie (oh, and a wife).

The night before, I read Omar the vows we would be making as part of the ceremony to ensure he understood them.

'"For richer, for poorer, in sickness and in health."'

'Yeah, but not too sick or too poor!' he interrupted. 'Can't I choose which vows I say and which I don't?'

'Behave yourself!'

In the event, he said his vows perfectly in the registry office in front of a crowd of friends and relatives: Tina, Carolyn, my brother Stephen, my uncle Paul, but unfortunately not my sister Gillian, who was working in New York at the time. Félix and all the guys from Raíces Cubanas were there with their wives and girlfriends, having arrived by coach early in the morning. Someone forgot shoes to wear with a suit and borrowed some from Omar, then hobbled around comically all day because they were three sizes too big. Lubie was the best man, and my brother took my arm and walked me into the registry office so that I didn't have to use a stick.

After the formal bit was over, everyone came back to my house for a party. It was a blazing-hot afternoon, which meant

I didn't have good control of my legs. I found a comfortable spot in the garden and let everyone come over to talk to me, and I managed to stand up for the wedding photos, albeit leaning on Omar's arm. It was a lovely atmosphere, with most of my neighbours there. The musicians started jamming and everyone joined in, either dancing or singing along.

That night we travelled to Leeds to watch Raíces Cubanas playing on stage. I sat in the DJ's box to the side, where I had a perfect view. When Félix announced to the crowd that it was our wedding day, everyone cheered and I felt like joining in.

All in all, having felt that I wasn't the marrying kind, my wedding day turned out to be one of the best days of my life. I'd always thought weddings were expensive shows for other people, not really my thing, but it was truly magical. I'm sure every bride feels the same way.

The day after the wedding we drove to Liverpool and got Omar's passport stamped with the right to live and work in the UK for a year. After that we had to wait a year for him to get permanent leave to remain, and then another year before he could apply for a British passport, which would make it a million times easier for him to travel. It was ridiculously complicated and time-consuming (not to mention expensive) getting all the visa requirements for a Cuban passport sorted. Most important to us, it meant that Omar could stay with me as I consulted doctors – not just about my MS, but also about another issue that was on my mind at the time: babies.

Chapter 9

The Baby Question

Being a married woman made me think back on my mum and dad's marriage, with all its complexities and strangeness. It's hard to understand how they ever came to get married in the first place, given that they were so different. How did Irene Barnard and Peter Purdy fall in love when they were such opposites? Separately they were wonderful people, but together they just didn't work.

My dad was an inventive and unconventional man who wanted to make an impact on the world through his designs. My mum gave birth to his five children and understandably wanted to know how she was going to feed them. She told me that once, when they were living in a caravan in Brighton and Dad was working as a photographer, he accidentally dropped his camera in the sea. He came home, his head buzzing with ideas about how he was going to dry it and clean out the salt, while she was devastated to see their one source of income drowning in a plastic bucket. He couldn't understand what she was yelling about or why she was so upset; he simply saw it as a challenge to be overcome. She couldn't understand why he wasn't as devastated as she was. They were at a complete impasse.

Dad needed a partner who would go somewhere new and exciting with him at the drop of a hat, whether it was to ride camels in the Sahara or take a balloon flight over the Amazon. Mum needed someone with a steady income so she could buy food for her children. She couldn't stand all the fluctuations in their fortunes because she was responsible for five little people. Sometimes Dad would make a decent amount of money and we'd all get new clothes and toys. Then, the following year, the house would be on the verge of being repossessed because they couldn't pay the mortgage. When he invented a new machine we were comfortably off for a while, but if he was embarking on a new project we'd be broke until he could make it work. He was interested in solving problems, not making money. Over the years he got the Queen's Award for Industry and was inducted into the American Inventors' Hall of Fame, but he never quite achieved financial security.

My parents were both wonderful people, but the turmoil of their marriage, from which neither got what they needed, made being good parents difficult. There were constant arguments in the house. I'm told they were in the middle of an argument when Mum went into labour with me and she never made it to the hospital, so the upshot was that Dad had to deliver me himself in the bedroom of our South London house. As the youngest, I think I was their last attempt at reconciliation, but it obviously didn't work.

All through my childhood I remember furious arguments and insults being hurled, supposedly out of earshot of the kids. When I was five, Carolyn and I were sitting huddled on the stairs eavesdropping on a row down in the sitting room when suddenly she lost her balance and fell. She cut her head on the banister and there was blood everywhere. Dad came charging out of the room and mistakenly thought that I must have pushed her, so he smacked me. It was the only time in my life that he ever hit me and the shock of it is still vivid in my memory. Up till then I'd been the spoiled baby of the family and it felt like a real turning point. I was devastated to have fallen from favour, even though Dad apologised to me later when he had calmed down.

They were both very intelligent people, but neither of my parents pushed me to do my homework or to stick at any hobbies or interests. They never worked as a team, so if Mum banned something I knew I could go to Dad and chances were he'd overrule the ban. That kind of inconsistency is baffling and unsettling for children. We were never short of food: Mum would have starved and gone naked before her babies went to bed hungry. One year my only Christmas present was some doll's clothes that Mum had hand-knitted, yet other years I'd get piles of presents if Dad had come into a bit of money. We never knew where we stood, and there was a lack of individual attention. Perhaps that's partly because five children is a lot for anyone to manage, but I think it's also because the volatile dynamic of the marriage was so distracting for them both.

When I was 12 Dad went to work in America. At first he was away for two weeks, then back for two months, then away for three months and back for a month, and then it was six months away and the gaps between seeing him got longer and longer. In fact he never came back to live permanently with Mum again. They didn't divorce, because he was loyal to his family in his own way. He and Mum could hurt one another enormously, but they had a strong commitment to each other as well. They just needed to be on separate continents with an ocean between them for their marriage to work!

No one ever explained anything about the situation to me or my siblings. I just accepted that my dad was away working. I certainly didn't think that my parents had broken up. It didn't occur to me to question our family living arrangements. Uncle Tony, a father of six children, was divorced, but this was never mentioned or explained. He also worked abroad and I assumed fathers usually worked in a different country. When it came to my dad, I accepted what I was told at face value, and that's why it came as such a surprise to me when I arrived in Norway in 1987, at the age of 24, to find that he had a girlfriend. He'd probably had girlfriends all along, because he was very sociable. I'm sure Mum was happier without him as well, though I don't think she ever had another man in her life: five children are enough without a grown-up one to deal with.

Dad's girlfriend, Eppy, once asked me why my mum and dad didn't divorce and I didn't know what to say. Eppy seemed worried that Dad wasn't being straight with her, but I genuinely think it was a sense of responsibility that stopped him from formally ending the marriage, rather than any lingering romantic attachment. I think it's a shame two such caring, intelligent people couldn't find a path to suit them both.

I decided that I wouldn't make a good parent given the poor example of parenting that we had grown up with. Tina had two kids, a boy and a girl, but Carolyn, Stephen and Gillian didn't have any. Then, in 1992, just after Mum's death, I made a very strange decision about my fertility. I had myself sterilised.

Mum had been a practical but emotional woman who didn't always have the tightest grip on reality. I felt so unstable after she died that I convinced myself that I was developing my own emotional problems. My memory was shot to pieces and I had a few symptoms that I now realise were probably MS-related: feeling my balance wasn't what it used to be and getting occasional pronounced twitches. I couldn't think clearly and solve problems rationally the way I used to, and it terrified me that things were happening I didn't understand. My GP referred me to a psychiatrist, who agreed that there were probably some mental health concerns. That's when I told them that I wanted to be sterilised. How could I bring up a child while I thought I was wrestling with a phenomenon I couldn't understand? I wanted to feel as though I was in control and I hadn't yet realised that life just isn't like that.

The doctors probably shouldn't have let me go through with the sterilisation. I was 29 years old, childless, single and had just lost my mother. I was also a strong-minded, articulate individual who had decided what she wanted. I'm very good at persuading people to do what I want them to do, and doctors aren't infallible. I told them I couldn't contemplate having a child when I suffered from mental health problems, that I'd never wanted to have children anyway, that I was positive this was what I wanted. I told them that if I ever felt able to raise a child, I would want to adopt. They agreed to tie my tubes. The operation was carried out on International Women's Day in March 1993.

Then, two years later, I met Omar, went on to marry him and the whole landscape changed.

While Omar and I were living together in Singapore back in 1996, my period didn't come one month and I convinced myself that I was pregnant. I assumed the fallopian tubes had reconnected themselves, which can happen in rare cases, and I had mixed emotions about it. Part of me felt it was too early in my relationship with Omar to be sure things would work out and that we'd stay together, and I felt strongly that children should have two committed parents. Another part of me, however, was delighted to think that we might have created a little person together. I surprised myself by how happy I was.

I was nervous when I first mentioned it to Omar. 'Erm, I'm not sure what's going on, but my period is two weeks late and it's never late and I'm beginning to wonder if ... you know ...' I'd told him back at the beginning that I wouldn't be able to get pregnant and we had both had Aids tests (easy and common in some parts of the world), so we had never used any contraception. 'We've only been together for a year, so it's too soon to think about having a baby. We don't know what's going to happen or where we'll be a year from now. What if we break up? That wouldn't be fair on a child.'

Omar grinned. 'What's with all the worrying? If the mother and the father both love a child, then it will grow up just fine.'

'So you would help to support us?'

'Of course I would! In Cuba men don't walk away from their children.'

'Do you want to have a child, though?'

'I'd love to have children – lots of them. And I'd like to have them with you.' He grinned again and gave me a hug.

My period came the following month, so I wasn't pregnant after all, but I now knew that Omar wanted to be a parent one day. His cards were on the table. I watched him whenever we were around other people's children and I could see what a fun daddy he would be. He let the kids climb all over him, carried them on his shoulders, told them stories or played funny tunes on his violin for them. He could have them absolutely spellbound. He wasn't a disciplinarian, though. I knew I would have been the one who made sure they did their homework and ate five portions of fruit and veg a day, but then I would have been happy to do that.

When we came to England, I started talking to social services about adoption. We discovered my MS would rule that out, as they didn't want kids who had potential problems of their own being placed with a disabled parent. I felt furious at the time, but I saw the sense in it a little later. I didn't want Omar to miss out on being a parent, but a couple of things stood in the way. First of all, I had to persuade the doctors to reverse my sterilisation, a procedure that is not always successful. After we got married in 1998 I went to my GP and asked for a referral to a surgeon.

'Have you thought through all the implications, Debbie?' he asked. 'For example, have you discussed with Omar what would happen if you weren't able to look after the child yourself?'

My MS diagnosis obviously put a huge spanner in the works. I had asked Omar how we would cope if I became too disabled to look after a child, and even how he would manage as a single parent if I died. His attitude, as always, was that we would deal with each situation as it arose.

'Don't fuss about problems that might never happen. What a waste of time that is!'

That was the extent of our discussion, but I managed to convince my GP and the specialist to whom he referred me that we had planned for every contingency. I was just as vocal and eloquent in persuading them to reverse my sterilisation as I had been in getting them to do it in the first place! The operation went ahead but was unsuccessful. We would have to consider other options.

Having explored adoption and reversal, the next step was IVF, but before the hospital would consider that route we had to have counselling to make sure we had considered all scenarios posed by my MS. We must have satisfied them because I was put on a course of hormone injections, the first step towards IVF. The odds were stacked against me: I had been sterilised, I had MS, and by that stage I was 36 years old, so I'd passed the watershed when women's fertility starts plummeting. We had to move quickly.

I didn't have the dexterity to give myself the hormone injections and I would have ended up divorcing Omar if he had tried to do them, so each day I went to a local hospital. They tested my hormone levels every couple of weeks and after six weeks they realised my ovaries had gone into overdrive. It was nice to know that part of me was still working efficiently. My legs were getting weaker by the day, I was finding it harder to read, and my hearing was deteriorating, but my ovaries were doing just fine. When they did the procedure to remove the eggs they got thirty-four viable ones out of my ovaries, while I believe the norm is eight or nine.

Now it was Omar's turn to do his bit. A young nurse gave him a plastic beaker and directed him to a little cubicle.

Originally they were going to implant the eggs in my womb on 9 September 1999. I was delighted with the choice of date: all the nines is very auspicious in the Chinese calendar. However, I had too much discomfort due to the overstimulation of my ovaries, so they delayed it until October and the three eggs they had been planning to use had to be frozen and then defrosted. It was late October when the procedure went ahead.

I knew that, whatever happened, Omar would be a fantastic father. Even if by any chance he and I didn't stay together in the future, he would never walk away from his child. He had a good relationship with his ex-wife and his ex-girlfriends and I was confident we would always be friends, so hopefully that would make us good parents as well. My parents had never been friends with each other; maybe that was part of the problem.

I waited two weeks before going back to hospital for a pregnancy test. We were both over the moon when it was positive. I really hadn't expected it to be, given that the odds were against me. It seemed like a miracle.

'Oh my God! Omar, you're going to be a daddy!'

He hugged me tightly and I think there was a tear in his eye, although he denies this point blank. 'That's my girl!' he whispered.

We were so happy that we rang all our friends and family to tell them. Everyone was overjoyed for us. At last things were starting to go right for me again. People promised to pass on cots and prams, baby baths and car seats. On a wave of excitement I rushed out and started buying baby clothes – the cutest little white and yellow cardigans and Babygros and bootees, as well as rattles and mobiles and cuddly toys. We even had preliminary discussions about a name, though we had no idea of the baby's sex.

When I was eleven weeks pregnant I went for a scan. The radiographer was all chatty as she helped me up on to the bed and spread the gel on my stomach, but then she went quiet.

'Is something wrong?' I asked.

Omar grasped my hand.

The safety point was twelve weeks: we only had a week to go.

'Just a minute,' she replied, frowning. She moved the transducer over my belly from side to side and I stayed very still, hardly daring to breathe. I knew something was wrong. What was it?

'I'm so sorry but I can't find a heartbeat,' she said at last.

'What does that mean?' Omar asked.

'I'll just go and get a doctor to come and talk to you.'

She left the room and Omar put his arms around me. Neither of us could speak, the disappointment was so great. No heartbeat must mean the baby was dead. I couldn't cry – not yet anyway.

The doctor confirmed that I'd had a miscarriage, but because I was taking hormone tablets I hadn't bled and lost the foetus that way. I stopped taking the pills and then the foetus came out. Unfortunately it wasn't totally expelled, so I had to have a D&C, in which the lining of the uterus is scraped. The whole experience was so painful. The pain wasn't in my body; it was in my heart.

Omar was devastated and unable to talk about it. I didn't want to talk either. It was too awful. I felt as though I had been given the best present in the world, and just when I was getting used to this wonderful gift it was snatched away from me, and I didn't know why. If only they had planted the eggs on 9 September, the auspicious date, they'd have been able to use fresh ones rather than frozen. That's all I could think. I felt as though I was letting Omar down, as though it was my fault our baby had died. It was because of my stupid body, with all its problems.

'There's no reason a subsequent pregnancy wouldn't work,' the doctor told us. 'Give it a break for a couple of months to allow you to recover physically and then we can try again with more of the eggs we've removed.'

That was something to cling on to. We could grieve for this baby and then try again.

We spent an awful evening calling everyone to tell them I'd lost the baby. Several friends cried because they were so upset for us. I sobbed the whole time because it was heartbreaking putting it into words: 'I've lost the baby.' It made it sound as though it was carelessness, as though I hadn't been looking after it well enough. We packed the baby clothes and toys away into a box so as not to tempt fate and vowed we would wait until well into the pregnancy before we told anyone next time.

The good news was that the viability of my eggs was high. They only freeze grades A and B, but I had loads of them, all frozen in little batches of four. To implant the next three, they would defrost a batch of four and see how many viable ones were available. The doctor's description made them sound like fish fingers instead of babies, but we listened hard to everything we were told and tried to stay positive. How could I not conceive with so many viable eggs?

We went through the whole process again. I lay on my back with my feet in stirrups as three fertilised eggs were implanted inside me, then waited two weeks. But the pregnancy test was negative.

'It's OK, sweetheart. We'll just try again,' Omar comforted me.

They defrosted another four eggs and we tried again. And again. And again. In all we had five attempts at IVF, but I never got pregnant after that first time. After every attempt there was that horrible, sickening moment when the test results came through negative. By that stage we'd used up all our viable eggs and couldn't afford to go through another cycle of ovary stimulation and egg removal, even if my health had been up to it.

I can't blame the MS. Lots of women with MS get pregnant and have healthy babies. If they have relapsing-remitting MS, they may find they have a relapse after the baby is born, but during pregnancy their body protects the foetus. Healthy women don't always conceive or carry to term through IVF. The bottom line is, it just didn't work for us.

We were both heartbroken that we would never be able to watch a child of ours growing up. I'd wanted Omar to have a little one whom he could teach to play the violin. I was heartbroken that I never got to hold the baby who was in my womb for those all-too-brief eleven weeks. I used to dream about that child and start crying in my sleep. I tried to keep my tears secret because I didn't want Omar to see how upset I was in case it made things harder for him.

When we talked about it after the initial grief had passed, though, we decided it was karma. It wasn't meant to be.

During the two years I spent trying to get pregnant, my health had deteriorated. It wasn't as a result of the hormone treatments or the pregnancy – just a natural progression of this disease that had taken up residence inside me like an unwelcome houseguest. The reason why we gave up after five IVF attempts was because I passed the stage when I would be able to get out of bed in the middle of the night to lift a crying baby from its cot, rock it and settle it down again. I was fast heading towards being a wheelchair user and unable to drive, so how would I have got our child to school if Omar was away playing a gig? How would I have managed bath-times? How could I have dressed a small, wriggling child when I had trouble dressing myself?

If the pregnancy had worked back in 1999, I could have managed to look after a baby then, but by 2001 I knew I wouldn't be able to. I was on a downhill slope and it was getting harder to look after myself all the time, never mind someone else.

Although I hadn't had the best parents in the world, I'd grown up with dozens of children around me in a big old house in Balham, South London. There were the five of us, and for a while Uncle Tony and Auntie Anne lived downstairs with their six kids, so we were two boys and nine girls in total, all within ten years of each other, and we usually just had our mothers around. The area was Irish and Caribbean, so big families were the norm and we all played together in a huge park at the end of the road. By nature I was a bit introverted, but you have to come out of your shell to make yourself heard in a crowd that size and I learned a level of social confidence that would stand me in good stead later. We had a lot of freedom from adults and that helped to nurture my independent spirit. You can never get too big for your boots, though, when you are the second youngest in an extended family of eleven kids, because someone will always be there to tease you out of it. All in all, it was a brilliant childhood. It didn't seem like it at the time, maybe not until MS made me think about what I really had, but now I can appreciate it I wouldn't change a minute of it.

As for having children ourselves, it wasn't meant to be. We'd done our best, but it hadn't worked. And so our dream of parenthood came to an end.

Chapter 10

The View from 4 Feet

I was walking at my wedding in 1998 and I was walking during my brief pregnancy in 1999, but it was becoming more of a struggle. One day I took Omar to the airport to catch a plane to Germany for a gig, and as we hurried to the terminal over an uneven surface I fell and twisted my knee. When I tried to stand up again it was extremely painful, so Omar put me on a luggage trolley and wheeled me into the terminal.

'I won't go. I'll cancel,' he said.

'Just get on the bloody plane. We need the money. I'll look after myself.'

At last he agreed to go, after I rang my sister Carolyn and she said she would come and pick me up. Her husband came as well to fetch our car. They drove me home, but I could barely climb the two steps to my front door and the pain was getting so bad that I called an ambulance. When we got to hospital they found that I had broken my leg, just below the knee. It's fortunate I had reduced sensation in my legs or I would have been in agony. Or it would have been fortunate, except that it was because of the reduced sensation that I didn't feel myself starting to twist the leg in an awkward way. A person with full sensation would probably have been able to stop themselves from falling at such an odd angle in the first place.

While I was in a cast, Vera came over from Oslo for a visit. I hired an automatic car so I could still show her around the area (probably not my best decision). Soon after the cast was taken off I was at home, at the top of my stairs, and turned round to speak to someone and the leg broke again. I couldn't believe it. It was back on with the cast and sitting with my foot up and struggling to hobble around for a few more weeks looking like a Weeble. ('Weebles wobble but they don't fall down.')

Throughout 2000 walking became increasingly difficult. I'd stagger from one place to another, clinging on to door-frames and handrails, and I had a few falls that could have been nasty. I already used the wheelchair whenever I had any distance to cover and by the end of the year I had accepted that I needed it more or less full-time to get around. I couldn't risk having any more breaks. It could be my back next time, not just a leg.

Most people were very supportive of my decision to use a wheelchair, but a few friends were horrified.

I went to meet a musician friend, a Cuban singer, at London's Waterloo Station one day. It's fully wheelchair-accessible there and I was wheeling myself around the concourse quite happily, but my friend's face fell when he saw me.

'Oh, no! Why are you in that thing?'

'It makes my life a lot easier, that's why!'

'If you give up you'll always be in the chair. You've got to keep fighting.'

I sighed. There are a number of misconceptions about wheelchair use. It's the disease I have that has made me lose my muscle strength, not using a wheelchair. Back when I first met Omar I was physically fit, but my muscles were losing their tone and definition long before I took to the chair because I just wasn't getting the amount of exercise I used to due to my MS. I could only walk for a limited distance without becoming exhausted, so I tended to avoid making journeys if I possibly could. For example, I could only manage to get to one or two shops before I needed a rest; once I was in a wheelchair I could wheel myself all the way round the shopping centre and get a lot more done.

I experienced circulatory problems as a result of having MS, not because I was in a wheelchair. I'm at increased risk of a deep vein thrombosis because I sit still so much of the time, but I was doing that anyway without the chair. The chair means I can sit still *and* get the shopping done. My spine has a tendency to hunch forwards, but not as badly as it was doing when I had to lean forwards on to walking sticks.

When I was 15 years old I had a boyfriend called Nelson who used a wheelchair, so I was familiar with some of the downsides as well as the advantages of seeing the world from 4 feet off the ground. I met Nelson while I was working as a volunteer for the Windsor and Maidenhead District Sports

Association for the Disabled (WAMDSAD). A number of Paralympic athletes trained there, so it was a very inspirational environment. The volunteers helped to set up sports equipment to enable the disabled athletes to get on with the sport. I also waved a bucket under people's noses on a number of fundraising wheelchair pushes.

Nelson had had a spinal accident some years before I met him. He was much older than me, in his 20s, and he was an exciting, fun person to go out with. He had a wicked sense of humour, an upbeat attitude and a healthy libido! I wasn't ready for a sexual relationship at 15, but that didn't stop him trying at every opportunity. He was a great example of someone who didn't see being in a wheelchair as a barrier between him and anything he wanted to do.

We went out with each other for about five months and I had plenty of time to witness the 'Does he take sugar?' attitude you can come across when you're in a chair. You know the kind of thing – you're in a coffee shop and the counter assistant asks the able-bodied helper how the wheelchair-user takes his coffee. It's a classic. People feel awkward because they can't easily look you in the eye when you are sitting down and they are standing up. While I was out with Nelson, people were forever asking me what he wanted. 'Ask *him*, for God's sake!' I'd reply testily. Times have changed, thankfully!

I'm quite a loud person, so I didn't have a problem with people talking over my head once I was in a wheelchair. I did feel guilty sometimes when people were getting cricks in their neck from bending down to talk to me, but I guess it's better than me getting pain from always looking up (selfish, but honest). My friends get used to it.

Some people are offensive to wheelchair users, in the same way that some people are offensive to women, or the elderly; it's not deliberate, just thoughtless. In fact I think the elderly have it worse than us because there's a sector of the population who assume that if you're over 65 you must have senile dementia. If elderly people stand at the side of a road they risk someone grabbing their arm and pulling them across, even if they hadn't wanted to go that way. Things have changed a lot for the disabled over the last twenty years or so, in the same way that they have changed for black people. There is more discussion and understanding of our needs, and there are far more laws on our side. Some people are still ignorant, but Rome wasn't built in a day.

I know some wheelchair users who have a militant attitude, daring anyone to discriminate against us and campaigning against shops and public places that don't offer suitable access. If people fail to make any effort to improve accessibility for the disabled because they don't care or don't want disabled patrons, they deserve to be harangued, but in my experience the problem is usually lack of understanding of how to be accessible. Sometimes regulations cause the 'sat-nav syndrome', meaning that when you engage regulations (or sat nav) it disengages the brain. I've had some positive experiences since using the chair: London cab drivers who take me a few hundred yards up the road when I'm too tired to push myself and then refuse to take a fare from me (yes, really!);

nurses who walk through snow to my home because the roads are treacherous and I can't get to hospital; and people who stop to push me in the street when I get tired. Life in a chair is undoubtedly fraught with obstacles, ignorance and patronising attitudes, but like many difficult journeys the view is breathtaking. Negotiating the difficulties can be heartbreaking and draining, but then you get a glimpse of the human spirit and you feel privileged to be a witness.

Omar just accepted me being in the chair, the same way he has accepted everything else about the disease. If it made my life easier, that was fine with him – although he did say that he missed being able to walk along the road holding hands with me. The things I miss most are dancing and playing sport, but there's no point pining for things you can't have. You have to live in the present rather than looking back.

It was tricky getting around in a wheelchair in my house because the front door opened into a tiny hallway – just a metre square – and the stairs led directly off it. To get to the bedroom and bathroom, which were both on the first floor, I had to park my wheelchair at the foot of the stairs, transfer across and haul myself up on my bottom. Unfortunately that meant the front door wouldn't open because my wheelchair would be blocking the way. If Omar came home from a gig when I was already in bed, he had to reach his hand round the door and stretch to shove the chair out of the way before he could get into the house. When I came back downstairs in the morning my chair wouldn't be there any more and I'd have to drag myself across the floor to reach it.

I was forever bumping into furniture as I wheeled myself around the house: knocking over cups, denting doors and furniture, and bashing my toes. I lost toenails on several occasions when I slammed into cupboards, which were at exactly the same height as my feet in wheelchair footrests. Fortunately I couldn't feel the pain, but there was blood everywhere and my feet began to look particularly unattractive as the nails grew back all warped and bumpy.

Right from the off I was determined not to let the wheelchair stop me going anywhere I wanted, whether I was on my own or with someone else. I had to remember the lesson I had learned in King's Cross Thameslink on that day back in 1997 – it doesn't diminish you to ask for help. People like to be asked when it is something they can manage; it makes them feel good to be able to help others.

I've only ever had one refusal when I've asked for a hand. I'd been to an exhibition in Earl's Court and was trying to get back to my hotel, but the camber on the pavement I was on was quite steep and I couldn't manage it under my own steam because my arms were aching after a long day propelling myself around. A businessman came by, swinging a briefcase, and I called out, 'Excuse me. Please could you give me a push?'

'I'm in too much of a hurry,' he muttered without looking at me, and rushed past.

I watched him go, my eyebrows raised in surprise. We were heading in the same direction, so it wouldn't have taken him out of his way.

A woman with heavy shopping bags had overheard. 'For goodness' sake!' she exclaimed. 'Can I help?' I took her shopping on my lap and she wheeled me briskly along the pavement. 'Are you all right from here? Want me to take you further?' she asked. I think it was easier to push me than carry the bags.

'No, thanks. That's great.'

When I was out with Omar and another friend, we got stuck at Streatham Station by a flight of stairs up to street level. Some Caribbean lads in hoodies got off a train and Omar called them over. 'Can you give me a hand getting my wife up these stairs?' They grabbed a corner of the chair each and lifted me to the top – no mean feat because the chair and me together weighed a good 100 kilos.

There can always be difficulties: shops with a ridge at the entrance that I can't get my chair over; friends I can't visit any more because their flats are on an upper floor without a lift; and hotels can be a particular problem. The Disability Discrimination Act requires all hotels to have rooms for the disabled, but that doesn't necessarily mean they have wheelchair access. Hotel owners might think the fact they have a lift makes everything accessible, but when you reach your room the doorway might have sharp turns to negotiate as you enter, or it's impossible to get into the toilet, or there is no space to pull the wheelchair up alongside the bed. Trying out a new hotel can be a lottery, but I've found enough good ones to keep me off the streets.

All kinds of buildings in London can be a challenge. Victorian and Georgian architects weren't thinking of wheelchair users when they put in all those tiny half-landings and kerbs and flights of steps up to the front door. Having said that, they are as nothing compared to the steep hill on which my home in Bradford is situated. There was no way I could get up and down it on my own before I got an electric wheelchair (and that wasn't until 2008). A couple of times when Omar and I have been bickering in the car on the way home, he has got me out of the car into my chair and threatened to push me down the hill. The first time he did that, I squealed loudly and several neighbours peered out at the disturbance. Since then I have to keep quiet so as not to cry wolf! I'm banking on the fact that he won't actually do it, but you can never be too sure!

Foreign travel is a bit of a gamble since I've been in the chair. You don't know when you might get stuck at the foot of a flight of steps, come upon a cobbled street or be unable to get access to a disabled toilet (and not be understood if you ask for help). Luckily Omar and I are able to go over to Oslo to stay with Vera, because her flat is totally wheelchair-accessible. It's a big, modern apartment with spacious rooms. Norway is generally a very wheelchair-friendly place (apart from the tram lines).

Vera had had a good friend called Karl who was in a wheel-chair after breaking his back in a road traffic accident, so she knew which restaurants and bars around the city were easy to negotiate, and which ones we shouldn't try because the tables were too close together or the loos were downstairs.

Omar enjoyed Norway because Vera's boyfriend was a musician, a piano player, and they sat jamming for hours on end. He was able to take long walks in the snowy mountains. Some kids even showed him how to toboggan (which proved useful in Bradford this January).

Being in a wheelchair hasn't changed the person I am. It gives me a few more physical challenges to overcome on a day-to-day basis, but it also gives me more freedom to get out and about than I had immediately before I started using it. I think some people are afraid that they will be patronised when they are in a chair, but I haven't found that to be the case. Perhaps it's because I'm so loud. I think maybe if you expect it, it's more likely to happen.

Wheelchair users are all different. There's Dame Tanni Grey-Thompson, who won sixteen medals at the Paralympics between 1988 and 2004, Stephen Hawking, who has done ground-breaking work on the physics of black holes, and 90-year-old grannies who sit in a nursing home watching daytime TV. Then there's me, who never liked physics and wouldn't take part in any wheelchair races unless you could use a Formula One electric chair. I am a bit of a News Channel junkie, though. (By an odd coincidence, three of the five able-bodied people who used to help at WAMDSAD when I did are now in wheelchairs – one from a stroke, one from a car accident and me from MS.)

None of us wheelchair users are the same. To imply that we are is like saying that all 25-year-olds are the same, or all blonds are the same. Disabled people vote for different political parties, have different religions and watch different television programmes in much the same proportions as able-bodied people do. We are not heroic, nor are we sub-human. We're just people. People who happen to get around on wheels.

Chapter 11

The Big Four

When I was first diagnosed with MS, after I'd got over the shock I was relieved to find that my strange mixture of symptoms had a known cause and I assumed that the doctors would have a raft of treatments to deal with them. It wasn't long before I realised that this was not necessarily the case. My life was going to change considerably and permanently, and there was nothing medical science could do about it.

My first concern was that I wouldn't be able to walk any more. I believed that my life was all about activity and mobility, and being in a wheelchair would fundamentally alter my identity. In the event, losing the ability to walk happened so gradually, over a period of years, that there was no major turning point, no moment when I broke down and sobbed at the loss. It wasn't easy staggering around with walking sticks and then taking to a wheelchair, but I can't remember a precise date when I found I could no longer walk at all.

There were other things that were hard as my mobility decreased. I had always enjoyed going out with friends, which often involved a couple of drinks, but I could no longer risk more than a glass of wine in case I fell over, which would have been embarrassing and possibly painful. I started to watch what I ate because I was afraid that if I did fall and someone had to pick me up they might drop me if I got too heavy. No more decadent Christmas lunches or hitting the brandy afterwards! I decided to cut right back on what I ate during the day so that I could afford to eat dinner with Omar in the evening.

Many of my greatest fears have been about embarrassment, and incontinence was definitely on that list. How did people manage when they couldn't control their own bowels and bladder? I'd been coping by not drinking anything when I wasn't going to be close to a toilet, and avoiding spicy foods that might precipitate an involuntary bowel movement. However, I was still having to take antibiotics for urinary-tract infections because my bladder wasn't emptying properly, so in 2000 a nurse showed me how to self-catheterise. I hated that, but only because it was embarrassing. It's not painful or even particularly difficult, but it is not something I'd pictured myself doing in my 30s.

I needed to plan outings around my bladder. If I had a drink before we left home, I had to be sure there was a loo I could use when I reached my destination. In all the years we've been together, the best present Omar has ever bought me was a RADAR key, which gives me access to most disabled toilets in the country. My planning ahead didn't always work, however.

Once Omar and I were driving to Asda to do our shopping when we got stuck in a traffic jam. I think there had been an accident because the traffic wasn't moving at all and I was conscious that I'd had a glass of juice before we set out, confident in the knowledge that Asda had disabled toilets. Unfortunately we sat and sat and suddenly the worst happened: I smelled that acrid smell and felt urine soaking through my trousers.

I burst into tears, but Omar was completely matter-of-fact about it, as usual. When we reached Asda he picked me up and carried me inside to the toilets, then left me to strip off and clean myself up while he got me some new knickers and pull-on tracksuit trousers from the clothing department. That was an embarrassing incident, but it taught me a useful lesson: never leave home without baby wipes and spare clothes.

Much as I hated self-catheterisation, when I found I was losing dexterity in my fingers and couldn't manage it any more, I was bereft. For a long period I wore incontinence pads, which have the advantage of being straightforward to use, but I always wished for a more discreet solution. Several doctors asked whether I wanted to have a permanent catheter fitted, but I assumed that this meant a urethral catheter and I imagined that it would get in the way of my sex life, so I always refused. I should have asked for more information.

Towards the end of 2007 I was stuck in bed with flu. I felt thirsty but couldn't drink anything because my high temperature affected my muscles and made it difficult to get myself to the toilet. I lay there feeling lousy and crying with frustration.

Just at the right moment a continence specialist arrived to see me and straight away she asked, 'Debbie, why have you rejected a supra-pubic catheter?'

'A supra what?'

I'd no idea that you could get a catheter inserted above the pubic bone, directly through your abdominal wall into the bladder. I was really excited about the idea and talked about it at a couple of patient groups of which I was a member, where I was surprised to find that some of the women had already had them for some time. Once we were talking about it, others decided to investigate it themselves. I went into hospital for an operation to have one fitted in January 2008 and found it incredibly liberating. At the same time as the catheter, I had a Mirena coil put in, which meant my periods became so light they were barely noticeable. Another lesson learned: ask questions and talk to people, even if the subject is embarrassing, and even if you think you know the answer already.

Bowel incontinence presented more of a problem than bladder, because there would be no way to hide the fact if I had an accident. Also, I was taking gradually increasing doses of painkillers containing codeine and morphine, both of which make you constipated, and the constipation is painful and causes intense headaches. None of the things you can take to relieve constipation give you 'control' of the problem and the whole situation was pretty frightening. I felt insecure leaving the house and decided to increase my dose of codeine if I was planning an outing anywhere. That's all I could think of, short of giving up on any kind of social life. This wasn't how I'd expected my life to pan out, but that's how it was.

By the end of 2008, eureka! Specialist continence nurses told me about a brand-new product called Peristeen, a personal colon-irrigation system that had become available on the NHS. It's a simple way for anyone to clean out their colon on a daily basis and so prevent accidents or constipation. In LA celebrities pay a fortune for colon irrigation as a health treatment. Peristeen is cheaper and without the glamour, but to me it is a priceless necessity that lets me continue to enjoy my life.

A big worry for any young person (and yes, I still consider myself in this category) diagnosed with a serious illness is bound to be sex. The actress and wheelchair user Julie Fernandez, who is best known for her role as Brenda in *The Office*, once wrote a funny and honest article about men's attitudes to her being in a wheelchair. She relates a story about a plumber who came to mend her sink and who thought it was OK to ask her if she is able to have sex!

I couldn't decide whether to be shocked or amused that a strange man would have the nerve to ask a pretty young actress such a thing, but I certainly had those worries for myself. As mobility and sensitivity diminish, it affects your sexuality, but sensuality and intimacy mean different things to different people. I think it's important always to consider what you *can* do, rather than mourn what you can't. Physical expressions of love and affection change throughout your life. Disability has affected my body but not my mind, and I've always thought the brain is the most erogenous zone.

If you find yourself in a wheelchair, the best advice is to look for a professional to whom you are comfortable talking. I'm terribly English and always blush when I talk about sex, but it's important to be able to ask a continence specialist or a neurologist or any healthcare professional whatever questions you might have and pinpoint the solution that will work best for you and suit your lifestyle. Omar is not remotely embarrassed about asking questions. When the occupational health people came round to teach me how to use a hoist to get out of bed by myself, he was in the bedroom with them busily discussing how it could be used as a sex toy, while I buried my crimson cheeks in my hands in the next room.

The fourth of my fears in the early years of having MS was that it would be painful. The headaches I got, like a hand stretching in and squeezing my brain, could be excruciating, but mercifully they were always brief. When I began taking daily painkillers, which I've done since 1998, I stopped being so aware of the headaches and I don't think I get them any more. I think they occurred as scleroses were forming in my brain and I'm not making any new ones now – it's just that the ones I have are getting bigger. (At least that's my theory.)

Other bits of me hurt, though. My legs swell up badly due to my poor circulation and that can be very painful. My back hurts, especially if I've been slumping in my chair. My arms and shoulders hurt when I've been wheeling myself around in a self-propelling chair. I get pains in my stomach sometimes. The drugs I take to deal with one symptom can have side effects that cause another problem. Sometimes I have to choose between the original symptom and the cure, weighing up which will be more debilitating in my life. Other people think they know what's best, but even the best-intentioned nurses, doctors, carers and husbands can't experience my life the way I do. I have to make decisions about what treatments are most appropriate for me, and these may not always be the best available. Everything is a balance and I need to find out for myself what I can cope with.

Those were my four biggest fears: immobility, incontinence, sex and pain. Then, in June 2001, I was watching the news when it was announced that someone called Diane Pretty, who was terminally ill with motor neurone disease, was taking a case to court asking the Director of Public Prosecutions to give her husband immunity from prosecution if he should ever help her to commit suicide. I was stunned. Couldn't people do that already? If not, why not? A whole new kind of worry entered my head.

Chapter 12

Let's Talk about Death

From the age of 16 until I was 23 I had an on-off boyfriend called Alex who was suffering from heart disease. He was diagnosed about six months after we met and told that he would be dead in two years if he didn't stop smoking, drinking and staying out late, start eating properly and taking gentle exercise – a lot of rules. He tried for about two months to live the life they wanted him to, but then he thought, Forget it! I'd rather have fun!

I was very much in awe of Alex. He was seven years older than me and a very strong, good person, the kind of person who makes a positive difference in the world. He was a social worker, aiming to improve his clients' lives in a very real sense. He was out there in the community, getting involved in projects like clearing waste ground to make a playing field for kids, cleaning up graffiti or fundraising for the elderly.

He had a strong sense of right and wrong. I remember once when we were in a pub, some aggressive bloke slapped his girlfriend in the face and split her lip open. Everyone saw it happen – they'd turned to watch because the couple were screaming at each other – but Alex was the only one who jumped to his feet and remonstrated with the guy. He didn't get thanked for it, though. The girl turned on him, shouting, 'Don't you dare threaten my man! Who do you think you are?' Alex was like that. If kids were kicking a football against someone's front door or chucking takeaway cartons on the ground, he would go up and confront them. He had a strong social conscience and would always stand up for anyone in need.

Katie, my best friend at college, used to go out with a lot of real idiots. She liked bad boys who gave her the run-around, but I found them stupid and uninteresting. Alex ticked all the boxes for me. He had strong left-wing values, he was intelligent, and he was black, meaning that my parents disapproved of the relationship – a definite plus for a rebellious 16-year-old. Mum and Dad weren't racist exactly. They'd have been hard pressed to put their finger on what they were worried about, but it was there. I think a lot of their generation who didn't grow up in a multicultural society remain uncomfortable around those of a different race, at least until they get to know them.

The reason my relationship with Alex was on-off was because he didn't want me to become too attached to him. I was at college and then university and he said I should be free to go out with other people when I wanted (as I'm sure he was doing). I think partly he didn't want me to get too involved because he knew his time was limited and he didn't want me to become dependent on him.

I did as he wanted: went to university, worked in the night-club in Birmingham, then took the Thomson Directories job before moving up to Scotland. I saw other men, but I always looked forward to the reunions with Alex, when he would travel up or I would travel down for a long weekend.

In 1986 I got the phone call I'd always dreaded. His mum rang to tell me he was in hospital and very poorly. 'I think it's the end, Debbie,' she said, so I caught a train down and rushed to his bedside. I got there in time to tell him that I loved him. His family and friends came in to say goodbye, and then his mum and I were by his side as he slipped into unconsciousness and died, at the age of 30. It couldn't have been more peaceful.

It was devastating for me, of course – my first real experience of the death of someone close apart from my grandmother Nana Ray – but I felt Alex had made the right decision. He spent the last six years living life to the full, knowing that he wouldn't ever reach the age of 40. He got four years more than the doctors had told him he would and he lived every single day of them to the maximum.

It was a civilised kind of death, in that it had been expected, discussed and planned for, and I saw how that made it easier for those he left behind. We missed him, of course, but there was no element of shock. He had made many friends as a trade unionist and they all turned up at his crowded funeral, along with family and other friends and clients, to celebrate a life well lived. There were tears, but everyone had had a chance to come to terms with his death and to say goodbye.

My siblings and I had gone to a C of E Sunday school when we lived in South London, but our parents weren't religious and I think they only sent us so that we would be able to make up our own minds. That and the fact that Father Woods used to walk through the neighbourhood collecting all the local children on Sunday mornings. By my late teens any faith in God had fizzled out, to be replaced by faith in Karl Marx. I don't think there is an afterlife or heavenly choirs – I believe that when you're dead you are worm food – so it makes sense to do the best you can while living on this earth.

There's only one thing I do now that appears religious (although it is actually superstitious) and that is every time I cross the Pennines at Saddleworth Moor I make the sign of the cross. Little Keith Bennett, victim of the Moors Murderers, Ian Brady and Myra Hindley, is still out there somewhere. It's a story I was told since I was knee-high and I always make the sign of the cross to respect and remember Keith.

Mum's death was completely different from Alex's: sudden, shocking and, as it turns out, untimely. If only someone had diagnosed her diabetes, it could have been controlled with medication and diet, just as my uncle Frank's always was. Instead the diabetes led to hydronephrosis of the kidneys, which led to heart failure.

I never expected Mum to die. I knew she wasn't well, but I still thought she would live for ever. She must have felt horrible most of the time, but she didn't whine or complain. Then she collapsed one day when Carolyn and her husband were there. They called an ambulance and she was rushed to hospital, but she was still chatting away and seemed perfectly fine when I spoke to her in hospital that evening.

The next day I phoned the ward from work to see how she was doing.

'We told you to get here,' a nurse said to me, sounding almost angry.

'No, you didn't,' I replied. She must have spoken to one of my sisters. 'Why? What's happened?'

She instructed me to get there as soon as I could and that's when I realised it was serious and my world fell apart. I knew I was too hysterical to drive, so I called a friend, who came and picked me up and took me to the hospital. When I got there I was told that Mum had died. Tina and Carolyn were there, and we just sat with Mum's body for ages, talking quietly to her, wanting to feel she was still with us.

We all reacted badly. None of us could believe it. Death just didn't happen in our family. The night she died we all sat at Carolyn's house, trying to work out how we should feel and what we should do. Mum hadn't left any funeral instructions and we couldn't decide between burial and cremation, and if so, where. She died in Bradford, and that's where Carolyn and I were living, but Tina lived in Nottingham, Stephen lived in London, Gillian and Dad were in America, and Mum originally came from Brighton, where most of her family still lived. The undertaker kept ringing and asking, 'What do you want us to do?' and no one could give him an answer. Each of us thought we knew best what Mum would have wanted, but our ideas were all different.

At last Dad stepped in and made the decisions: it was to be a cremation, and the funeral would be held down in Brighton. We didn't decide what to do with the ashes and I kept them for years before we buried them in the same grave as her mother. Her family agreed we could do that.

Having seen the turmoil and additional grief the disagreements caused us, Dad wrote his funeral wishes in detail shortly afterwards. He stipulated where he was to be cremated, the kind of coffin he wanted, the hymn that was to be sung – 'All Things Bright and Beautiful' – how it was to be paid for and what he wanted to happen to his ashes. Dad wasn't morbid – he was very much a glass half-full person – and he wanted his funeral to be a celebration, thus the unconventional musical choice.

I learned a lesson from his forward planning. We have a big problem in modern society in that we don't talk about our deaths, so our loved ones are left guessing our wishes after the event. It's a problem for those who need organ transplants as well. Not many families sit down and discuss it, so when there is a fatal road accident and the next-of-kin are still in total shock, they don't know what to do when a doctor comes along asking if they've ever thought about organ donation. The decision needs to be made within an hour or so of death and few people are ready for it.

Dad did us a great favour by taking the decision-making out of our hands. His death was awful, horrible, terrible at the time, because there hadn't been any warning at all, but we just had to turn up at his funeral and focus on our own emotional state.

I think we all felt bereft when we became orphans. It doesn't matter what age you are when it happens. Tina was 40 years old by then, but she said the same thing. I was so glad that I'd had that period living with Dad in Norway, and I'd also gone to visit him when I was in the States, as well as staying with him midweek when I lived in Redditch from 1993 to 1994. It was comforting to know I'd spent some time with him in his last years.

The other comfort was that he knew nothing about it. He went to bed, had a heart attack and didn't suffer. Same with his brother, Tony, and sister, Judy, who went within weeks of him. I think I spent a few months in shock afterwards, though. I didn't even start grieving because I couldn't believe what had happened. It felt completely unreal.

Just over three months after Dad died, I met Omar. I wish with all my heart they could have met in the flesh, because I know they would have got on. One was an inventor, the other is a musician, but they both had the souls of improvisers.

Losing his father and his elder brother within a year of each other while Omar was in his early 20s must have been awful for him, especially as he then took on the weight of responsibility for the family. He'd been brought up in the Cuban religion of Santería, a faith of African origin. Because he has African heritage on his father's side and native Cuban on his mother's, Christianity never seemed appropriate. He keeps an altar in his office with a glass of water, a flower, a candle and some photographs and he will go there to meditate and focus on the day ahead, but it's more of an important superstition than a religious faith.

Like me, he doesn't believe in an afterlife. His mother died in 2008 and he still talks to her sometimes in his head, while sitting at his altar, but that doesn't mean he thinks she can hear him. It's just a comforting ritual. After my mum died, I kept picking up the phone and dialling her number and getting a shock when the number was unobtainable. It's hard to let go when you are used to a regular communication with someone. Your brain can't seem to get used to it.

As family and friends passed away over the years, I realised that any of us could die at any time. Omar could get knocked over by a bus on his way back from a gig. My brother or sisters could die suddenly. I might seem vulnerable because I have primary-progressive MS, but I could outlive them. Life is unpredictable, and all you can do to make it easier to cope for those you leave behind is to talk about what you want to happen in the event of your death. That's what Diane Pretty was doing when I heard her on the television news. She was quite reasonably asking the courts to let her decide how, when and where she would die.

Like me, she was in a wheelchair. Like me, she had an incurable disease. She had motor neurone disease, which is a terminal illness, and I had MS, which isn't, but right from the start I was worried that her fight would have consequences for me one day.

was such clear common sense. I knew that you could request a 'do not resuscitate' notice, so that medical staff don't intervene if you have heart failure, and I'd heard that doctors will give lethal doses of morphine, knowing it will kill patients, if that dose is necessary to stop the pain. What was the moral difference? What did it serve anyone to keep Diane Pretty alive to the bitter end?

Outside the courtroom, Diane and Brian announced straight away that they were going to appeal. But was there enough time? Her condition was deteriorating fast. I went over and over the problem in my head. If I found myself in the same situation, would I have to wait until I choked to death? Couldn't anyone help me to die peacefully and painlessly? And then it came to me: I was fairly sure they had voluntary euthanasia in Holland. Would that be a solution? I Googled and found an entry for an organisation called the Voluntary Euthanasia Society, so I called them up and got a nice lady on the other end. I was sniffing back tears as I spoke.

'Hello. I've been following the case of Diane Pretty and I'm scared because I've got MS and I'm worried I might be in the same boat one day. Surely there's something that you can do without being prosecuted. Isn't there a way round it?'

'I'm sorry,' the lady said, 'but I'm not allowed to give you advice on this. It would be illegal if I told you what can be done, regardless of whether you plan to do it or not.'

'But that's crazy!'

'The law is very unclear. It's a kind of catch-all type of law that says it's illegal to counsel, procure, aid or abet the suicide

Chapter 13

The Speeding Train

Diane Pretty was an attractive, blonde 41-year-old mother of two when she was diagnosed with motor neurone disease in 1999. It was devastating news, and her doctors could offer her little comfort. Around 50 per cent of sufferers die within fourteen months of being diagnosed, and the vast majority are dead five years later, although there are exceptions still alive twenty years on, notably Stephen Hawking.

As the name suggests, motor neurone disease attacks the nerve cells that control the movement of muscles, and as the disease takes hold, sufferers have trouble walking, then the paralysis spreads till they can't move in any way – can't speak, can't swallow. Sufferers sometimes die when the diaphragm becomes paralysed and they can no longer breathe – in other words, they suffocate, and that's what Diane Pretty was most scared of.

By the time I saw her on television, Diane was paralysed from the neck down, sitting propped up in a wheelchair, and her speech was very slurred and difficult to make out. As she described her fear of suffocation, I felt a crawling sensation all over my skin – I had had choking fits on a couple of occasions just before that and they were utterly terrifying.

Omar was out when I had the first one. I hadn't been eating or drinking anything. I think a dribble of saliva got down my windpipe and suddenly I was bent over coughing myself scarlet in the face, wheezing deeply and unable to catch my breath. I panicked because there was nothing I could do – no way I could attract the attention of my neighbours in the street or phone an ambulance – because I couldn't talk. For a terrifying minute I tried everything I could think of to clear my windpipe to no avail, until one final, painful cough cleared the obstruction and I slumped, exhausted from the effort, my chest tight and sore and my heart beating hard.

I could understand why Diane Pretty was scared of this. It would be a horrible way to die. No one would wish it on an animal.

The TV news explained that under the terms of the Suicide Act 1961, the last legislation on the subject that was passed in Britain, it's not against the law to commit suicide, but it is a criminal offence for anyone to help you. Diane was long past the point when she would have been able to do it for herself, but if her husband, Brian, helped her he risked prosecution. It seemed ridiculous and obviously wrong. It was one of these examples of outdated laws that somehow got overlooked on the statute books, like the ones forbidding you from driving herds of cattle over Westminster Bridge or playing football on a Sunday unless you've done two hours of archery practice first.

They went to court and Diane's lawyer argued th[at] 2 and 8 of the European Convention on Huma[n] which protects the right to private and family life, w[as] contravened if her husband wasn't allowed to end he[r] ing by helping her to die.

Brian accompanied Diane to court every day. When a[jour]nalist asked him if he agreed with Diane's battle, he sa[id] haven't had my own way in twenty-five years of marri[age] What makes you think I'm going to get it now?'

'Huh! I know how he feels,' grunted Omar.

That's what I liked about the Prettys. They seemed like [a] normal couple, the kind of people I would have liked to ge[t] to know. Brian wasn't wrapping her up in cotton wool and trying to do everything for her. He just did what needed to be done. She wasn't anything like the normal image you might have of a suicidal person – she seemed to have a great sense of humour despite the fact that she had been struck down by this dreadful disease and was trying to deal with it as best she could. What conversations had she and Brian had with each other behind closed doors? How much heart-searching had there been? What did their children, Brian and Clara, who were in their 20s, think of it all? I watched every bulletin, waiting for the news that I hoped would give Diane the verdict she wanted, so that she could be allowed to die in a dignified way in her own home.

The courts refused her application, saying that while Article 2 gives a right to life, it doesn't give the right to die peacefully. I was horrified. How could that be? Diane's request of another, punishable by fourteen years in jail. That means that if you even talk to someone contemplating suicide and don't attempt to talk them out of it, you could be breaking the law. The net is thrown really wide.'

'I could still go to Holland, though, couldn't I? They allow it there.'

'Under certain, very limited circumstances they do,' she said doubtfully, 'but it's not an easy option.'

I couldn't rest until I found a solution, so I rang directory enquiries and asked for the Dutch Embassy. When I got through to an official, I questioned him. 'Is it true that you have voluntary euthanasia in your country?'

'Yes,' he replied warily, 'but there are lots of provisos and safeguards.'

'What kind of provisos?'

'I'm not a legal expert, but the person would have to be in unbearable mental or physical pain, be of sound mind when they made the decision and be able to prove it was their choice and no one had pressured them to make it.'

'And after that, does a doctor help you to commit suicide?'

'A doctor would be involved in discussing the decision with the patient and then in prescribing the correct drugs.'

That all sounded humane and reasonable. 'So what would I do if I wanted to commit suicide in Holland? How would I go about it?'

There was a long pause. The guy obviously thought he'd got a madwoman on the phone. 'Do you live in Holland?' he asked eventually.

'No.'

'Are you registered with a Dutch doctor?'

'No.'

'I'm afraid you would need to satisfy the residency criteria, then get yourself registered with a doctor before you could be given any help of this kind.'

'How long would I have to be resident?'

'I'm not sure about that. Probably a year. Do you want me to find out?'

'Yes. Thank you.'

He continued, 'But you would then have to make sure that the doctor you were registered with supported euthanasia. They don't all do it.'

'Couldn't I ask how the doctor felt about it before I registered?'

'That's not how it works.'

So it sounded as though Holland wasn't an easy option, but I decided that I might consider registering with a Dutch doctor as an insurance policy. I'd probably have to pop over from time to time for check-ups, but I've always liked Holland and at that time there was a £9.99 direct flight from Leeds Bradford Airport to Schiphol. As my mum used to say, prepare for the worst, hope for the best and expect something in between. The Dutch option wouldn't work for Diane Pretty, though, because by the sound of things she might well not have a year left.

I watched with interest as she went to the High Court and then the Court of Appeal, but each time the judges, while

Chapter 13

The Speeding Train

Diane Pretty was an attractive, blonde 41-year-old mother of two when she was diagnosed with motor neurone disease in 1999. It was devastating news, and her doctors could offer her little comfort. Around 50 per cent of sufferers die within fourteen months of being diagnosed, and the vast majority are dead five years later, although there are exceptions still alive twenty years on, notably Stephen Hawking.

As the name suggests, motor neurone disease attacks the nerve cells that control the movement of muscles, and as the disease takes hold, sufferers have trouble walking, then the paralysis spreads till they can't move in any way – can't speak, can't swallow. Sufferers sometimes die when the diaphragm becomes paralysed and they can no longer breathe – in other words, they suffocate, and that's what Diane Pretty was most scared of.

By the time I saw her on television, Diane was paralysed from the neck down, sitting propped up in a wheelchair, and her speech was very slurred and difficult to make out. As she described her fear of suffocation, I felt a crawling sensation all over my skin – I had had choking fits on a couple of occasions just before that and they were utterly terrifying.

Omar was out when I had the first one. I hadn't been eating or drinking anything. I think a dribble of saliva got down my windpipe and suddenly I was bent over coughing myself scarlet in the face, wheezing deeply and unable to catch my breath. I panicked because there was nothing I could do – no way I could attract the attention of my neighbours in the street or phone an ambulance – because I couldn't talk. For a terrifying minute I tried everything I could think of to clear my windpipe to no avail, until one final, painful cough cleared the obstruction and I slumped, exhausted from the effort, my chest tight and sore and my heart beating hard.

I could understand why Diane Pretty was scared of this. It would be a horrible way to die. No one would wish it on an animal.

The TV news explained that under the terms of the Suicide Act 1961, the last legislation on the subject that was passed in Britain, it's not against the law to commit suicide, but it is a criminal offence for anyone to help you. Diane was long past the point when she would have been able to do it for herself, but if her husband, Brian, helped her he risked prosecution. It seemed ridiculous and obviously wrong. It was one of these examples of outdated laws that somehow got overlooked on the statute books, like the ones forbidding you from driving herds of cattle over Westminster Bridge or playing football on a Sunday unless you've done two hours of archery practice first.

They went to court and Diane's lawyer argued that Articles 2 and 8 of the European Convention on Human Rights, which protects the right to private and family life, would be contravened if her husband wasn't allowed to end her suffering by helping her to die.

Brian accompanied Diane to court every day. When a journalist asked him if he agreed with Diane's battle, he said, 'I haven't had my own way in twenty-five years of marriage. What makes you think I'm going to get it now?'

'Huh! I know how he feels,' grunted Omar.

That's what I liked about the Prettys. They seemed like a normal couple, the kind of people I would have liked to get to know. Brian wasn't wrapping her up in cotton wool and trying to do everything for her. He just did what needed to be done. She wasn't anything like the normal image you might have of a suicidal person – she seemed to have a great sense of humour despite the fact that she had been struck down by this dreadful disease and was trying to deal with it as best she could. What conversations had she and Brian had with each other behind closed doors? How much heart-searching had there been? What did their children, Brian and Clara, who were in their 20s, think of it all? I watched every bulletin, waiting for the news that I hoped would give Diane the verdict she wanted, so that she could be allowed to die in a dignified way in her own home.

The courts refused her application, saying that while Article 2 gives a right to life, it doesn't give the right to die peacefully. I was horrified. How could that be? Diane's request was such clear common sense. I knew that you could request a 'do not resuscitate' notice, so that medical staff don't intervene if you have heart failure, and I'd heard that doctors will give lethal doses of morphine, knowing it will kill patients, if that dose is necessary to stop the pain. What was the moral difference? What did it serve anyone to keep Diane Pretty alive to the bitter end?

Outside the courtroom, Diane and Brian announced straight away that they were going to appeal. But was there enough time? Her condition was deteriorating fast. I went over and over the problem in my head. If I found myself in the same situation, would I have to wait until I choked to death? Couldn't anyone help me to die peacefully and painlessly? And then it came to me: I was fairly sure they had voluntary euthanasia in Holland. Would that be a solution? I Googled and found an entry for an organisation called the Voluntary Euthanasia Society, so I called them up and got a nice lady on the other end. I was sniffing back tears as I spoke.

'Hello. I've been following the case of Diane Pretty and I'm scared because I've got MS and I'm worried I might be in the same boat one day. Surely there's something that you can do without being prosecuted. Isn't there a way round it?'

'I'm sorry,' the lady said, 'but I'm not allowed to give you advice on this. It would be illegal if I told you what can be done, regardless of whether you plan to do it or not.'

'But that's crazy!'

'The law is very unclear. It's a kind of catch-all type of law that says it's illegal to counsel, procure, aid or abet the suicide of another, punishable by fourteen years in jail. That means that if you even talk to someone contemplating suicide and don't attempt to talk them out of it, you could be breaking the law. The net is thrown really wide.'

'I could still go to Holland, though, couldn't I? They allow it there.'

'Under certain, very limited circumstances they do,' she said doubtfully, 'but it's not an easy option.'

I couldn't rest until I found a solution, so I rang directory enquiries and asked for the Dutch Embassy. When I got through to an official, I questioned him. 'Is it true that you have voluntary euthanasia in your country?'

'Yes,' he replied warily, 'but there are lots of provisos and safeguards.'

'What kind of provisos?'

'I'm not a legal expert, but the person would have to be in unbearable mental or physical pain, be of sound mind when they made the decision and be able to prove it was their choice and no one had pressured them to make it.'

'And after that, does a doctor help you to commit suicide?'

'A doctor would be involved in discussing the decision with the patient and then in prescribing the correct drugs.'

That all sounded humane and reasonable. 'So what would I do if I wanted to commit suicide in Holland? How would I go about it?'

There was a long pause. The guy obviously thought he'd got a madwoman on the phone. 'Do you live in Holland?' he asked eventually.

'No.'

'Are you registered with a Dutch doctor?'

'No.'

'I'm afraid you would need to satisfy the residency criteria, then get yourself registered with a doctor before you could be given any help of this kind.'

'How long would I have to be resident?'

'I'm not sure about that. Probably a year. Do you want me to find out?'

'Yes. Thank you.'

He continued, 'But you would then have to make sure that the doctor you were registered with supported euthanasia. They don't all do it.'

'Couldn't I ask how the doctor felt about it before I registered?'

'That's not how it works.'

So it sounded as though Holland wasn't an easy option, but I decided that I might consider registering with a Dutch doctor as an insurance policy. I'd probably have to pop over from time to time for check-ups, but I've always liked Holland and at that time there was a £9.99 direct flight from Leeds Bradford Airport to Schiphol. As my mum used to say, prepare for the worst, hope for the best and expect something in between. The Dutch option wouldn't work for Diane Pretty, though, because by the sound of things she might well not have a year left.

I watched with interest as she went to the High Court and then the Court of Appeal, but each time the judges, while

Top: Meeting Omar's family for the first time in Havana, January 1998. From left to right are Victor, Gloria, Aaron and Ramses.
Insert: Omar's mother, Gloria. A little female version of him.
Bottom: A feast for the return of the prodigal son.

Top left: Omar with the legendary 'Mambo King', Señor Tito Puente (no relation).
Top right: Omar and the first incarnation of Raíces Cubanas.
Bottom: The Cuban Boys' Cuban girls!

The boys with Kirsty MacColl, February 1998. The beginning of a beautiful friendship.

Omar and the Missus. The top half of this picture was used for promotional shots. If only they could have seen the bottom!

Top: 14 May 1998. The first day of the rest of my life.
Bottom: It wasn't elaborate or expensive, but it was a great excuse for a party.

Cutting the cake, supplied by our
wonderful neighbour, Trisha.

Does my bum look big in this?

October 2008, arriving full of hope at the High Court.

With Saimo, Omar, Davina and Sarah: talking to the press after the appeal was rejected.

Disappointment after the High Court judgment.

30 July 2009, inside the
House of Lords: a tearful
Jo and stunned Sarah
help us to celebrate
a historic judgment.

I've got my life back! I
smiled so much that day,
my cheeks hurt.

sympathetic, said they couldn't give Brian what amounted to permission to kill her. It would set a precedent, they kept repeating. The Director of Public Prosecutions, Sir David Calvert-Smith, refused to rule out prosecuting Brian Pretty if he helped her to die in any way.

'We'll fight on,' Brian announced to the waiting media. 'We'll go to the European Court of Human Rights.'

By this stage his wife could only speak with the aid of an artificial voice synthesiser. 'I just want my rights,' she said, in her new electronic voice.

Diane looked so frail that day that I wasn't sure she would make it, and she nearly didn't. In March 2002, by the time the case came up in Strasbourg, she had to travel there in a private ambulance, accompanied by paramedics and an intensive-care nurse for the twelve-hour journey.

Interviewed outside the court, Brian said, 'It's very poignant that our very first trip abroad is to come here and argue for Diane's right to die.'

Diane sat with her head twisted to the side, following everything with her eyes. How brave to put herself into the media spotlight instead of staying at home and giving up, I thought. I already had days when I couldn't face going out because my legs hurt too much, or my shoulders were too stiff, or I just didn't feel up to it mentally. She must be in constant discomfort, yet still she persevered.

In court, her lawyer argued that to force her to die a distressing and inhumane death was against the European Convention on Human Rights, which guarantees respect for private life and bans degrading treatment. The UK's Suicide Act 1961 doesn't distinguish between those physically capable of taking their own life and those who are not, which could be seen to breach European rules on discrimination against the disabled because those not able to carry out the completely legal act themselves are unable to ask for help to do so.

The arguments continued and I followed the debate closely, keeping the news on in the background as I did the housework, booked gigs and train tickets for Omar, and carried on with daily life.

When the verdict was announced in April 2002, it found against the Prettys. The Strasbourg judges said that while Article 8 probably *was* engaged, Britain had a right to maintain a law that was contrary to the European Convention on Human Rights as long as it could be justified, as it always had been on the grounds that the Suicide Act was there to protect the elderly and vulnerable from abuse, and that building an exemption into the law would seriously undermine that protection. They upheld the UK court's decision that Brian couldn't help her to die.

Diane was in tears as they emerged from court, but she still managed to find a wan smile for the cameras at the press conference.

'The law has taken away all my rights,' she said, in her electronic voice.

That had been their last chance, the last hope of reprieve, and her supporters had hoped it would work. In the same month a British judge had given permission for doctors to withdraw all medical support from a woman known only as Miss B for legal reasons. She had asked to be allowed to die peacefully, and after being taken off a ventilator that she required for life support she did die, in her sleep. What was the difference between that and what Diane Pretty was asking for? Not very much, as far as I could see.

Only two weeks later my blood froze when I switched on the headline news of the morning to hear that Diane had died in a hospice in exactly the way she had feared. She had had breathing difficulties and spent her last days of consciousness choking and struggling for breath before she slipped, mercifully, into a coma and died a few days later.

During her last weeks a team from the BBC's *Panorama* had been filming in the Prettys' household to give viewers an idea of what Diane's life was like. It was very disturbing viewing.

The reporter asked, 'Isn't life always preferable to death?'

Diane replied via her voice synthesiser, 'I am dead.'

'Don't you have any quality of life?'

'What life?' she replied.

Inside, there was no mental deterioration. A brain as sharp as it had always been was working away, but she needed other people to do every physical thing for her; feeding, cleaning, sucking saliva from her throat and scratching her nose if it itched. In the last weeks of her life Diane would howl whenever she wanted something and Brian had to try and work out what she needed.

When she died, he emotionally told the media that she was 'free at last'.

I couldn't believe that in the twenty-first century any human being should have to suffer like that. It terrified me to think something similar could happen to me, even though the two diseases aren't the same. I was truly felled by the case.

Having motor neurone disease is like standing on a railroad track at a point where you can see a train roaring towards you at 100 miles an hour. MS is not a death sentence. I might have been standing on the track and able to hear a train somewhere in the distance, but I didn't know where it was or how fast it was approaching. Would it be able to stop before it reached me, or would I face the same fate as Diane? Since my diagnosis I had done my best to avoid thinking about the future, but now one possible future scenario had been portrayed for me and it was so horrific that I knew I had to find an alternative.

Chapter 14

Cuban Roots

'Omar, do you think you would want to commit suicide if your life became unbearable, the way Diane Pretty's was?'

'Oh my God, why do you have to discuss these things?'

'But would you?'

'Maybe. I don't know. It would depend.'

'Depend on what?'

'Depend on whether I had a nagging wife who was trying to make me have crazy conversations all the time.'

I tried again later. 'What elements do you think are essential for quality of life? I mean, if you'd asked me when I was 20, I'd have said I didn't think it would be worth living if I was stuck in a wheelchair and couldn't play sports, but now that I'm in a wheelchair it's absolutely fine. In some ways I'm glad it happened because I get to see a whole different side of life.'

'Uh-huh.'

I could tell I didn't have Omar's full attention, but I persevered. 'So you never know what compensations you might find. I mean, I would hate not being able to communicate what I was thinking, but maybe when that happened I would find I still had enough quality of life in other ways.'

'Maybe I would have a better quality of life if you couldn't communicate what you were thinking,' he said, somewhat rudely.

'How about you? How do you think you would feel if you went deaf and couldn't listen to music or play any more?'

'That would be bad. That would be very bad.'

I'm with him there, because music has always been important to me. I loved music as a kid and was introduced to jazz while at college in London in the early 1980s. There was a club called the Bass Clef right in the middle of the area that is now super-trendy Hoxton but in those days was a barren district of office buildings where all the lights went out at 5.30. The Bass Clef must have had a great manager because they booked real musicians playing real music. Among the artistes I remember seeing were the great South African saxophonist Dudu Pukwana and a very young Courtney Pine.

Ronnie Scott got a much-deserved OBE for services to music in 1981. He was the first UK promoter who made it possible for Cuban musicians like Arturo Sandoval and Chucho Valdés to come over and play in London, and Ronnie went to Havana in 1993 to co-host the Cuban Jazz Festival. Then, in 1998, Cuban music exploded on the world scene with the release of the Buena Vista Social Club album, and Wim Wenders's movie about those venerable musicians came out the following year.

Lots of the jobs I had on my travels round the world involved music in one way or another. Some great musicians hung out at the Café de Paris in Oslo and I met more through Mildred Jones; there was my work with her on sorting out her music copyrights, and there was the dancing job in Tokyo's Roppongi district. I must admit that I really miss dancing. When I listen to a great sound I can still feel the rhythm in my bones, but I can't get my body to recreate it. I can try, but my arms and hands don't move in time any more, so I look idiotic. I enjoyed writing for *Music Monthly* in Singapore, but my true baptism of fire came in managing Omar and his bands.

At least when I lived in the same house as the Cuban Boys I could shoo them all out through the door in time for a gig and make sure no one left their instruments behind. When I started managing Raíces Cubanas from our home in Bradford, that's when I truly earned my spurs! These guys lived in different parts of the country, so if I arranged a gig for them in Birmingham I had to work out transportation for each of them and send them the details. I didn't often travel with them, but I'd be sitting at home with the landline phone and my mobile ready to find out where they were if a club manager called to say they were late for a sound check. Before long I started booking their tickets for them as well. I could get cheaper deals booking online with a credit card, so more of the profit from the gigs went into their pockets.

What used to drive me crazy was when they would switch off their mobile phones so that I couldn't nag them. Definitely not the best way to get Debbie on your side. Finally, after much grief, they learned that life got a whole lot easier if they texted me when they reached the train station and texted me when they arrived at the destination. If I'm not worried, their lives, on the whole, will be much easier. It took a while, but like Pavlov's dog they got there in the end.

Once our keyboard player turned up in Sheffield and found that his keyboard was broken, so I had to borrow one from a local shop; another time he didn't turn up at all for the Window on the World Festival in Newcastle and Omar had to play keyboard instead of violin that day. There were always problems to be overcome. Fortunately Omar, along with the rest of the band, can play virtually any instrument that's put in front of him or we'd have had to cancel gigs a few times.

It's always hard to break into a new music scene and the fact that Omar played the violin didn't seem to help because in the UK it wasn't seen as a traditional jazz instrument in the way that the saxophone was and is. He'd call up a venue and the conversation would go something like this:

'Where are you from?'

'Cuba.'

'Great! And what instrument do you play?'

'Violin.'

'Oh, yeah? We'll call you if we can use you.'

There's a tradition of violin-playing in loads of other coun- tries – Ireland, Hungary, China – but in the UK it was seen as part of an orchestra and very much a classical instrument. Nigel Kennedy worked miracles in putting the violin on the map, first with his stunning recording of Vivaldi's *Four Seasons* in 1989, with which he made his name, and then in 1999 with *The Kennedy Experience*, which features his versions of Jimi Hendrix songs, but there is still a long way to go.

On Valentine's Day 1998 Omar's career received a boost when he met Kirsty MacColl, a musician famous for several Top 20 hits, including 'There's a Guy Works Down the Chip Shop Swears He's Elvis', 'A New England', 'They Don't Know' (most famously sung by Tracey Ullman) and 'Fairytale of New York' (sung with the Pogues). She was an active member of the Cuba Solidarity Campaign, a group that protests against the US blockade of Cuba and all the negative international press the Cuban government attracts.

She was going to perform at an 'I Love Cuba' event in London, and when told that we were putting together Raíces Cubanas she offered to sing a couple of numbers with them, so that there would be a seamless changeover from her set.

'Kirsty MacWho?' Omar asked when I first told him, and I had to explain.

Omar and I were invited for dinner at Kirsty's West London house to discuss how the concert would pan out. She cooked and we sat in her big kitchen with its red plastic chilli fairy lights and talked about Cuba Solidarity and how Omar was finding it in the UK. After eating, Omar played piano while she sang, and it was a privilege to be a fly on the wall, listening in.

Omar was amused that I was so deferential around her because I was a bit star-struck at first. He related to her as one musician to another without any awareness of her history, and I think that's why they hit it off so well.

Kirsty was a good friend of Cuba and after that first event she collaborated with lots of the guys from Raíces Cubanas, using them as session musicians on her last album. She decided she would like to learn how to play *tres*, the Latin-strung guitar, and paid our friend Leonel to teach her at a time when he was very short of money. She was also instrumental in helping Omar to meet music contacts here in the UK.

It wasn't charity. She didn't throw money around – that would have been insulting and patronising – but when Raíces Cubanas got a gig at Ronnie Scott's famous London club Kirsty rang some of her music-journalist friends and told them they should be there because this would be unmissable. She turned up herself and sat in with the band for a couple of numbers, knowing that her presence would bring them kudos. She also introduced them to officials from her record company and club owners who could help them. She couldn't have been more generous with her time and her connections.

More than this, on a personal level she became a good friend of ours. We stayed in her West London home when Omar had a gig in the capital, because I couldn't have slept on people's couches. She even gave us a spare key in case we ever needed to get in when she wasn't there. She opened her home, her heart and her fridge to us. As soon as we arrived, she would ask, 'Is anyone hungry?' If she and Omar were working together, I would often prepare some sandwiches and bring them in, feeling immensely lucky to be able to listen to these two incredible musicians doing their thing.

We began to housesit for her when she went on holiday. I was starting to use my wheelchair more when I travelled away from home, but fortunately Kirsty's house was wheelchair-accessible. My brother lived not far away, but his home was difficult for me to get into, so he came to visit us at Kirsty's instead. Omar and I enjoyed our stays in London and went to lots of gigs.

Omar played on Kirsty's last album, *Tropical Brainstorm*, which is heavily influenced by Latin American sounds. I loved the whole thing and laughed out loud at the track 'England 2, Colombia 0', which was about Latin men's relationships to women, something I had observed at first-hand.

Needless to say, she'd had an 'experience' with a Latin man herself along the way. We talked about our love lives once and she confessed to me, 'I don't need a husband – I need a wife!' I think she felt she needed someone in her life doing what I was doing for Omar. She'd got divorced from the father of her sons in 1995, so I was delighted for her when, in 1999, she fell in love with a musician and teacher called James Knight.

In December 2000 Omar and I were beside ourselves with shock and grief when we woke up to the news that Kirsty had been killed in a horrific accident in Cozumel, Mexico. She'd been diving in the warm turquoise waters with her sons when a speeding motorboat appeared from nowhere, coming straight towards them. She just had time to push 15-year-old Jamie out of the way when it struck and killed her instantly. It was an appalling, senseless tragedy that took on sinister overtones as the full story emerged.

The motorboat that hit Kirsty was owned by a Mexican millionaire, who was on board at the time of the accident. He claimed that one of his employees had been driving and that they had been travelling at a reasonable speed of one knot. The case went to court and the employee got off with a fine equivalent to about £60 in lieu of a prison sentence, as well as damages of US$2,150, payable to the MacColl family. However, several witnesses claim there was a cover-up and that the employee named hadn't been driving – someone else was at the wheel, someone not experienced at driving such a big boat, and that that person was going at speeds well over the one knot claimed and in waters reserved for divers, where it shouldn't have been. It was all controversial, bitter and horribly sad. Kirsty's mother, Jean, started a campaign to get justice for Kirsty. It would have given the family more peace if the whole truth had come out.

We were floored by her death for a long time. For Kirsty's mother, her boys, the waste of such a colossal talent and the loss of a wonderful friend. Without her, Omar's career in the UK would have been much slower to take off and we'll always be grateful for everything she did for us. I still have a key to her house. I suppose I should have sent it back but it feels like a little symbol of the affection and trust she offered us from the word go.

I wasn't well enough to travel by 2003, but Omar went to Cuba with Kirsty's mum, her sons and some other friends to scatter her ashes. They chartered a boat and sailed out to sea off Havana, the first time her son Louis had been out on the water since his mother died. Omar was playing a song he had written for Kirsty as they opened the casket to let the ashes fly off in the Caribbean breeze. Suddenly a flying fish leaped out of the water just by the boat and began to follow them. Flying fish aren't common in that part of the world, but this one stuck with them for hundreds of yards, clear for all to see. There's a picture of a flying fish on the cover of Kirsty's last album and Omar says it felt as if she was there. They could all feel her presence and it was beautiful.

It was after Kirsty died, when we were reading the sleeve notes of *Tropical Brainstorm*, that we realised she had thanked Omar and me in there. I can understand Omar being included, because he played violin brilliantly on the album, but it was lovely of her to include me.

Partly through working with Kirsty, Omar came to the attention of some of the UK's best-known jazz promoters and began to get more support-act and session work. Gradually he was moving away from his Latin roots and becoming more immersed in the jazz world, because that's where our worlds and musical tastes collided. He had an incredible break in 2004 when Courtney Pine got in touch, having heard about him on the musicians' grapevine. The brilliant young musician I had heard at the Bass Clef back in the 1980s had by then created a huge, enthusiastic following with his uniquely original contemporary jazz. When trombonist Dennis Rollins left the Courtney Pine Band, Courtney needed a new musician. He was experimenting with different line-ups so I was thrilled when he and Omar hit it off so well that he invited him to play and see how it went. According to Omar, this was like a masterclass for him, because they were all such brilliant musicians and Courtney is a great band leader who gives everyone their individual space. Through Courtney, Omar has done some gigs with Nigel Kennedy and come to the notice of many more people than he would have otherwise. He has also found a new family in the UK.

Living with a musician is a luxury. Sometimes he goes to his studio upstairs and plays for hours on end, and no matter what kind of day I'm having my mood is lifted as I listen. The violin is such a romantic instrument that it never fails to make me relax. Omar knows this and takes advantage.

'When I want to get into Debbie's bed, I just have to play violin,' he tells people, and it's true (although he forgets to mention the effect of twelve hours' practising the same tune).

One Christmas when we were very broke we agreed we wouldn't buy any presents for each other. Instead Omar woke me up on Christmas morning playing me a song he had written for me, which is now called 'Somebody Backstage' – the most romantic present I've ever had.

When he is playing a gig I am always the last person he talks to before he goes on stage, when I tell him, 'Go kill 'em, cowboy,' and after he comes off I am the first person he wants to discuss it with. If I can't be there in person, we do it by telephone.

Chapter 15

A Negotiated Settlement

As the MS started throwing up more and more symptoms, there were days when going to a concert was more than I could manage. They don't call it 'progressive' for nothing. As I look back I can see that every year I lost a little bit more control over my body. I was on a steady downward slope with an unchanging gradient. If I started the year at one point on the hill, by the end of the year I'd be just a bit further down. There was no let-up, no remission, just an inexorable downwards slide. I didn't wake up in the morning to find it was worse than the day before. It was only when I looked back and thought, Twelve years ago I was jumping out of aeroplanes and eight years ago I was scuba-diving, that it hit home.

By 2003 when I got tired my voice would start to slur, making me sound as though I was on my third glass of wine, and I would droop a bit to one side like a wilting flower. My fingers were losing dexterity, which meant I could no longer struggle into some of my best clothes without help. Fastening and unfastening buttons was out of the question, and I had trouble with zips or hooks and eyes, so it became hard to do up a bra on my own (not a good situation when you have big boobs and have just reached your 40th birthday: my mobility wasn't the only thing on a downward trajectory).

I became prone to dropping cups, phones and pens unless I concentrated really hard on gripping them. Before our stockpile of crockery became totally depleted, Omar started taking cups and glasses from me as soon as my hand began to shake. Then we bought plastic ones for when he wasn't there. He banned me from using sharp knives in the kitchen after a number of chopping accidents in which I was lucky not to lose a finger. I was a bit cack-handed when lifting things out of the oven as well and could no longer be trusted doing the ironing (as you can imagine, I was really devastated about that) after burning myself too many times. It was upsetting the day I found I couldn't put my earrings on any more. I've got lots of lovely little earrings, many of them from the jewellery stall I ran in Oslo in 1987, but my fingers weren't steady enough to get them through my ears.

The spasms that arched my back and made my legs kick and shudder became more frequent and, on the doctor's advice, I tried a couple of antispasmodic drugs – Gabapentin and Baclofen – but you're not supposed to drink when you're on them and I felt a bit woolly-headed. I was a little nauseous, so I had to take another drug to combat that. After a few weeks I decided the drugs weren't for me yet. When I got spasms I learned ways to move through them. They never last very long anyway.

Another bizarre side effect was that I stopped producing so much saliva, which gave me a really dry mouth and stale breath. The doctor prescribed a fake saliva spray, but it's the same consistency as saliva and I found it unpleasant to use – like coating your mouth in frogspawn. I decided instead to chew gum to stimulate saliva production. (I must look like an American teenager.)

I continued to avoid drinking too many liquids because I didn't want to spend the day hauling myself up- and down-stairs to the toilet. As my arms got weaker, we installed a commode in our kitchen – a cumbersome and embarrassing necessity made of metal and brown institutional plastic that looked like a cheap kitchen chair with a bucket underneath. Ugly, and in the kitchen!

The fatigue with multiple sclerosis can be just monumental. If there were an Olympic event that involved sleeping, I'd be a frontrunner for gold. Some days I am just too exhausted to go to the effort of getting myself up and ready to face the world. Little things like brushing my teeth seem Herculean tasks and it is easier to lie in bed with the news on in the background, drifting in and out of sleep, but putting the world to rights in between.

Omar wouldn't coddle me with sympathy – that's never been his style. Instead, if I have moments when I am succumbing to self-pity, he'll say something typically modest, such as, 'It's not that bad, woman. At least you've got me for a husband!' And I think he's right, although of course I don't say it (his ego is healthy enough as it is).

When you see someone on TV who is very disabled, you might think, God, I couldn't carry on if things got like that, but you can never genuinely walk in someone else's shoes (or roll on their wheels). Perhaps a young person would look at me and think, I'd never be able to cope with her life. Maybe it would be harder if you were younger and hadn't already realised some of your dreams, or maybe it's harder if you know what you've lost. I don't know, but for me, my physical problems don't make the world tiny, they just make it a different shape, and over the years I've adapted to that new shape. I call it a negotiated settlement – one in which the terms are renegotiated from time to time, as necessary.

Someone gave me the audiobook of Michael J. Fox's memoir *Lucky Man*, in which he tells the story of his experiences with Parkinson's disease. I loved it for its humour, its warmth and its total lack of self-pity. Michael actually says that if he were given the choice to relive his life without getting Parkinson's, he wouldn't take it. He considers everything that came with the disease to have enriched his existence. I know what he means. He's not resigned to having Parkinson's – if a cure were found he would grab it with both hands – but he would not have missed the experience he has been through. I feel the same way. All sorts of things have happened to me since I was diagnosed with MS in 1995. I've learned so much about the world and my place in it, and I've unlearned a lot of what I thought I knew.

My neurologist once told me that if a doctor is asked to rank someone's quality of life they will often rank it lower than the patient themselves would. Some doctors will see what they *can* do that you *can't*, rather than what you can do or experience better than them. People can't help looking at things from their own perspective. I've found that usually every negative comes with a positive and we just aren't always aware of it. It can take a lot of searching.

Society seeks perfection. If you can sing, you've got to be a multi-million-selling pop star; if you can act, you've got to have a mantelpiece full of Oscars. We all want wrinkle-free skin and airbrushed perfection, instead of healthy, normal flaws. I like the flaws: they're what make us interesting. Through all the symptoms of MS – the weak grip, the swollen legs, the dodgy eyes and hearing, the spasms – I can be more myself than I was before I was diagnosed. In many ways it's made me into a more worthwhile, interesting person than the girl who flitted around nightclubs and beaches in the Far East.

Although I was coming to terms with the disease, I hadn't yet fully 'accepted' it. Omar had been playing at a holiday show and had collected lots of brochures on diving for the disabled. All of them were in the south of England, a few hundred miles from home and so a bit complicated, but for the first time they made me look properly into disabled sports. My weak arms made things like wheelchair racing, basketball and tennis impossible, but I found that in Rotherham there is a reservoir where you can waterski in a sit-ski – skis that would accommodate a wheelchair user. We went there for our wedding anniversary in 2005. You can get snow sit-skis as well. If I'd known about these tools earlier, I would have been able to participate in sports that I loved for much longer than I thought.

The waterskiing was fantastic, and when Omar saw how much I was enjoying it he decided to have a go himself. Big mistake! The boat turned sharply, his weight leaned sideways, and while trying to keep himself upright he pulled some tendons in his arm.

Now, if I were to pull tendons in my arm it wouldn't matter. In fact I probably wouldn't even notice I'd done it. For Omar, though, it meant he couldn't play the violin for three whole months while they healed. Rather than sitting at home not earning money, he accepted invitations to sing with Latin bands. Most musicians wanted him to play violin, but his stage presence and vocals could not be underestimated. When one door closes, you need to find another way to do what you want.

Omar wrote 'Swings and Roundabouts' inspired by the massive culture shock he experienced when he first came to live in the UK and had to adjust to a place where there was snow on the ground, where he was separated from his family and old friends, and where people say, 'Please, please, please, thank you, thank you, thank you, sorry, sorry, sorry,' all the time. Gradually he made new friends and played with some amazing musicians who changed his musical style and he found that there are loads of benefits to life in England – not least of which, I hope, is being with me! I'd say that MS is my example of 'swings and roundabouts': for everything I have lost, there has been something to gain. I've just had to look pretty hard sometimes.

Chapter 16

A Short Stay in Switzerland

In January 2003 an organisation was reported in the media for the first time with a name that has since become a byword for suicide: Dignitas. A Liverpool man named Reg Crew, who suffered from motor neurone disease, had travelled to a clinic in Switzerland to be helped to die because the symptoms of the disease had become unbearable for him. He was only the second British person to use Dignitas and the first one the media had covered.

His wife, Win, and his daughter, Jan, went with him to Switzerland once he had become quite clear that he had only a bleak future ahead of him and was determined to end his life. He would rather have committed suicide at home, Win said, but he couldn't do it himself because he was paralysed from the neck down. They were too scared of prosecution to help him, and also scared of bungling it and increasing his suffering. So they travelled to Dignitas and were by his side as he passed away peacefully, and with dignity.

On her return to the UK, Win found that the police wanted to talk to her about her husband's death. She was interviewed at length and then she had to wait nine months to find out whether she would face prosecution and a prison sentence of up to fourteen years. All she did was accompany her husband to Switzerland so he could be assisted in dying in the way that he wanted. In the end the Director of Public Prosecutions decided not to press charges against this brave woman, who was in her 70s. The 'public interest' wouldn't be served, he said. But how had it been served by putting her through nine months of uncertainty, at a time when she should have been allowed to grieve the death of her beloved husband? How could it be considered in anyone's interest for Reg to have to travel thousands of miles, instead of being able to die in the comfort of his own home with his family around him?

The newspapers printed photos of Win and Reg at their wedding back in the post-war years, young and attractive with their lives ahead of them, and then of Win sitting beside her paralysed husband, propped up in a chair.

'Reg used to be quite sporty,' she said, 'but in the end he couldn't even hold his own head up. It was terrible for him. I watched him disintegrate, but although everything else had gone his brain was as sharp as ever. He knew everything that was happening to him.' Win had been brought up as a Catholic, she said, but ultimately she knew that it was right to help Reg to end his suffering, despite the leaders of the Catholic Church being vociferously opposed to assisted dying.

I looked up Dignitas on the internet and found that it is run by a lawyer called Ludwig Minelli, who believes that he is helping people to 'die with dignity' (thus the clinic's Orwellian name). There is no law explicitly permitting assisted suicide in Switzerland, but assisting in the suicide of someone who is suffering and wants help to die is not illegal, providing that the assister's motivations are selfless.

When patients arrive at the Dignitas clinic in Zurich, they are examined by a doctor to make sure they do indeed have the medical condition they claim, and to ensure that they are of sound mind and capable of making the decision. If they pass these tests, a doctor supplies them with a lethal dose of barbiturates, as a drink or a drip. The aim is that they perform the final act themselves – either swallowing the drink or turning the tap on the drip – if at all possible. As the lethal dose is handed over, the staff are very clear, saying, 'If you drink this, you will die.' It sounded eminently civilised to me – apart from the fact that the seriously ill person had to travel to Switzerland to get this service. Why couldn't they do it at home?

Once it entered my radar, I kept noticing news stories about chronically ill people and the terrible dilemmas they faced at the end of their lives. In May 2003 54-year-old John Close, another motor neurone disease sufferer, was taken to Dignitas by his sister, Lesley. She said he had planned his death for some time and had even held a farewell party for friends in the local pub. Describing his final moments, she said, 'He was able to press the plunger himself. We held his hands as a deep sleep became a very, very peaceful death.'

On her return, Lesley wrote to the police telling them what had happened and asking if she would face prosecution. After a long wait she was told that it was not in the public interest to take her to trial. Until then, on top of her grieving for her brother, she had had that additional concern about her own liberty.

I began to bend Omar's ear about it, just because it seemed so ludicrous and unnecessarily cruel. 'What do you think of this new Swiss clinic?' I asked.

He grunted non-committally.

'Don't you think it's only right that people should be allowed to end their lives when they are suffering too much?'

I rang the Voluntary Euthanasia Society to ask them what doctors are allowed to do here in the UK.

'There's a strange double standard,' I was told. 'Say you have two patients, both of whom are suffering unbearably with cancer. If one of them says to the doctor, "I want to die. Please help me," and the doctor then administers a lethal dose of morphine, that is illegal and the doctor could face fourteen years in jail for assisting a suicide. If, however, the doctor prescribes an increased dose of morphine to the other patient to relieve his suffering, knowing that it will probably prove fatal, then the doctor wouldn't have broken the law. So the patient who didn't ask to die can be helped but not the other.'

'That's ridiculous!'

'It's known as "double effect". If the doctor's main intention when increasing medication is to relieve pain, that's fine, even if it causes death, but if their intention is to cause death, they're breaking the law.'

While I was still on the phone, I was looking on the internet and immediately found Jack Kevorkian, an American right-to-die activist who claims to have helped nearly 100 people to end their lives using a machine he devised called the Thanatron, which delivers lethal intravenous drugs at the touch of a button, and the Mercitron, a gas mask that fills with carbon monoxide. He was arrested in 1998 and charged with murder after he filmed one of his assisted suicides and dared the authorities to take action. He spent some time in prison before being paroled, and his medical licence was revoked.

Despite my growing belief that people with an incurable illness should be able to end their lives peacefully, there was something distasteful about Kevorkian's grandiose self-publicity and his science-fiction-style suicide machines. I don't think assisted suicide should be turned into an industry like this, and in my view he probably did a disservice to responsible campaigners, like the Voluntary Euthanasia Society.

In Australia, Dr Philip Nitschke has helped a number of people to die. His approach is less sensationalist than Dr Kevorkian's, but he still produces books and holds seminars advising people on how to kill themselves, and he has made his own suicide devices, including the Exit Bag. I am fairly sure he has good motives, but it worries me that people have to pay for his products. As soon as there is profit involved, it feels wrong to me. I don't think suicide devices should be available freely via the internet to people who haven't received any counselling. That would mean it would be readily available to anyone in a temporary depression brought on by circumstances that would pass given time or the right support.

In the UK, the whole debate was muddied in 2004 by the actions of Yorkshire GP Harold Shipman, who is believed to have killed up to 250 of his elderly patients with lethal injections. People keep bringing up his name in connection with assisted suicide, but as far as I am concerned that is like calling Sweeney Todd a hairdresser! Shipman was a psychopathic murderer who was killing people who didn't want to die, whereas properly regulated physician-assisted dying should involve a doctor alleviating the suffering of someone who has no chance of recovery, at a stage when their quality of life is no longer acceptable to them. They're entirely different things.

While we live in a world where evil people like Harold Shipman manage to get medical licences, do we really want a system in which doctors can take the final life or death decisions upon themselves? That's the situation at the moment. If we had a law on assisted dying, chances are that Harold Shipman would have been caught sooner than he was because the system would have flagged up the number of people dying under his care.

Everyone has the right to ask not to be resuscitated in the event of cardiac or respiratory arrest, so long as they are certifiably sane. This seems eminently sensible. The problem is that doctors sometimes make 'do not resuscitate' decisions without consulting the patient, and this doesn't seem right to me. With legally binding 'living wills', we can make our own advance decisions that we want to be allowed to die under certain defined circumstances – for example, if we are chronically ill, incurable and life has become intolerable. Unless they have a heart attack, the bed-bound hospital patient's only option is to refuse treatment, food and water, and die a long, drawn-out death, suffering excruciating stomach cramps and other painful symptoms.

I became so obsessed with reading up on assisted dying that Omar got fed up with it. 'If you don't give it a rest, I'll buy you a one-way ticket to Switzerland,' he threatened, and it became a standing joke between us. When I nagged him about playing his violin late at night, when he might disturb the neighbours, he'd snap, 'You want that ticket to Zurich?'

Behind all the joking, I was genuinely scared that this might be an option I'd have to consider one day. I didn't want to die the way that Diane Pretty had died, or live the way she had lived in her final months. But what if I needed help to do it? The law was way out of step with the reality of people's lives in the twenty-first century and needed to be changed. They'd already legalised assisted dying in Holland and Belgium. The US state of Oregon had passed a Death with Dignity Act back in 1994, and the neighbouring state of Washington followed in 2008. Luxembourg had also created a law. Surely Britain would catch up before too long?

The Voluntary Euthanasia Society told me that a man called Lord Joffe was working on a bill, so I decided to wait and see what transpired.

Chapter 17

Entering the Fray

Joel Goodman Joffe is a Labour peer who worked as a human rights lawyer in South Africa in the late 1950s and early 1960s; he defended Nelson Mandela at his trial in 1964. In 1965 he moved to the UK, where he has done several jobs, including being chairman of Oxfam. In 2002, in the wake of Diane Pretty's death, Lord Joffe proposed a bill that would allow those suffering unbearably to request medical help to die. They'd have to make this request in writing, witnessed by a solicitor who could confirm that they were of sound mind. Doctors wouldn't have to assist if they didn't want to – it was a matter of conscience.

That's reasonable, I thought. How could anyone possibly be against it? A national opinion poll at the time showed that 81 per cent of the public thought that a terminally ill person who was suffering unbearably should be able to request medical help to end their life. The Royal College of Physicians dropped their previous resistance and adopted a position of neutrality on the issue, and to me that's the only safe position for any medical body to take. Surely assisted dying shouldn't be offered routinely as an alternative medical strategy, but neither should patients who have decided to explore the option feel abandoned by their healthcare professionals.

Evidence coming from Holland and Oregon showed that their assisted suicide laws were being used in only a tiny proportion of cases and there were no signs of them being abused. In Oregon, for example, only 1 in 700 terminally ill patients was choosing assisted dying, and the vast majority of them had been enrolled in palliative care first. Despite the evidence, there was vociferous opposition to Lord Joffe's bill from several directions.

Many adopted what they called a pro-life argument, saying that people could be pressured into ending their lives prematurely, but in response Lord Joffe pointed out that extensive surveys had shown that carers wanted the people they cared for to stay alive. He said, 'The key to it is that the people who would ask for assisted dying are independent and used to being in control of their own decisions in their own lives.'

Church leaders spoke out against the bill, saying that only God had the right to decide when to take a life (tell that to the Iraqis!). Bishops, rabbis, cardinals and imams, in a rare show of unity, spent millions of pounds to defeat Lord Joffe's bill and, to my astonishment, it was thrown out in 2003.

Lord Joffe came straight back with an amended bill that autumn, which restricted the bill to cover terminally ill people only. People would already have to be dying before their death could be hastened, so effectively they were just choosing a good death over a bad one. Wouldn't that silence the opposition's arguments?

Unfortunately, like most private members' bills that are introduced without government backing, this one was also thrown out, but only after an eight-hour debate in the House of Lords in which seventy-five different peers of all shades of opinion stood up to talk. There was a lot of discussion about whether the bill would lead to voluntary euthanasia, in which the doctor actually administers the lethal injection or drugs, as opposed to just issuing a prescription, which was the bill's intention. At least the debate meant people were starting to think seriously about the issue.

In December 2003 there was a tragic case that in my opinion highlights the need for serious legislation. Sue Lawson's MS had progressed to a stage that she found unbearable, and from which she could see no hope of relief. She couldn't walk, get to the toilet unaided or eat without choking. She decided to end her own life by taking a mixture of pills and suffocating herself with a plastic bag. Her brother, Graham, sat by her side talking to her and holding her hand for twenty-eight hours while her body struggled against her attempts. Although the pills made her woozy, the body's instinct for life is so strong that at the last moment she couldn't help pulling the bag away from her face and gasping for breath. It took many, many attempts before she finally fell unconscious and slipped away.

Graham's description of her last hours was heart-breaking to read and it was obviously a devastating experience for them both. He could have hastened her death by holding the bag in place, but she didn't want him to be directly responsible. Who would?

As soon as he was sure his sister was dead, Graham called her GP. The GP reported it as a suspicious death and Graham was arrested, taken to a police station, strip-searched and held in a cell overnight. Their parents had to hear the news of Sue's death from a police officer instead of their own son. Graham waited five months before being told that he wouldn't be charged. The family were finally able to bury Sue, as her body was then released by the police.

'She should not have died like that,' Graham said afterwards. 'No human being should. I feel honoured to have been asked by her to be there, but the fact that she could not have an easier death makes me very angry.'

It scared me when I read about Sue's final hours: firstly because her MS had made her decide that she couldn't bear living, and secondly because I realised how difficult it is to die by your own hand. If you take an overdose of pills, you might throw them up before they take effect, or you might live but with debilitating organ damage. If you throw yourself off a cliff, you might end up alive but even more damaged than you were before. Hanging might paralyse you from the neck down without killing you. The medical profession has access to drugs that can make death painless, swift and easy, but there are no infallible methods available to the general public. What kind of society would make Sue Lawson struggle for twenty-eight hours as she did?

I was brought up with a strong sense of right and wrong. I can only remember getting into trouble at school once, when I was very young and wrote my name on a wall in chalk. Obviously, if I'd been an experienced troublemaker I'd have thought through the fact that I was bound to get found out, and maybe have written something other than my name, but in the heat of the moment I didn't. Our teacher called me to come and stand at the front of the class, and I hung my head in shame as she berated me for 'vandalism'. I was so upset I told Mum and Dad about it that evening, convinced I was about to be expelled from school, and I remember their disappointment was almost tangible.

My sister Carolyn once stole a penny chew from a shop and was so stricken with remorse that she sneaked back later and left tuppence on their front step. It was winter time and when we passed the next day we saw that the coin had frozen to the step. She never stole anything again, and I never wrote on another wall.

'You don't let other people down,' Dad used to say. (It's ironic, really, since I'm sure Mum would say that he was forever letting her down.)

This moral sense definitely fed into my political beliefs. Maggie Thatcher was elected on 3 May 1979, the day before my 16th birthday, and I remember being devastated. I spent the next few years marching, demonstrating, standing on picket lines, handing out leaflets and chanting, 'Maggie, Maggie, Maggie. Out! Out! Out!' I collected money to support the miners during the long miners' strike of 1984/5, and I refused to go to A&E one night after hurting my finger so badly in a lift door that the bone was sticking out, because it would have meant crossing a picket line at the local hospital.

A long time has passed since those days, but I still get fired up about anything I think is unfair, and the more I learned about the outdated laws, the more incensed I became. What constituted 'aiding and abetting, counselling and procuring' a suicide? No one really knew. Would they prosecute the guard who pushed me on to a train on the way to Switzerland, or the chemist who sold me the paracetamol? It wasn't even clear whether a person had to be aware of the intent to commit suicide in order to be charged, so in theory someone could have aided and abetted without realising it. It was idiotic.

Lord Joffe's bill went backwards and forwards through the revision stages, hounded at every turn by the opposition lobby. The influential British Medical Association came out against it, but research shows that doctors admit to hastening the deaths of 3,000 patients every year for compassionate reasons (this is out of 500,000 recorded deaths in the UK every year). They were crying out for clarification of the law for fear of facing prosecution themselves.

'We should be focusing on increasing the quality of palliative care available to people who need it,' some lobbyists said, and Lord Joffe agreed with them. He argued for extra government funding for the hospice movement and palliative-care measures in general, and said he wouldn't be proposing his bill if he felt it would diminish the quantity and quality of palliative care available in any way.

Yet still the opposition raged. Cardinal Cormac Murphy-O'Connor, Archbishop of Westminster, warned that it could lead to pressure on vulnerable people to take their own lives. The Reverend Dr Rowan Williams, Archbishop of Canterbury, said that the cost of voting the bill through would be 'disproportionately high' compared to the benefit to a few individuals. And the pro-life lobby said, 'Legislation that permits doctors to assist in suicide fundamentally changes the role of doctor from someone who cures or cares to a killer.'

I sat at home yelling abuse at my television screen, using language I can't repeat here. Vulnerable groups were not suffering in countries where assisted dying was legal; in fact people were better protected by legislation. If one person suffers an unnecessarily horrible death against their will, then we should be doing something about it, and I thought that the doctors' oath was to first, 'do no harm', not keep everyone alive for as long as they possibly could.

A small but vocal minority within the churches talked about the 'negative message' we were sending to society about death, and I yelled, 'It's not a message! It's a human life!' According to their view, it doesn't matter how much an individual might suffer so long as the correct message is put across. That means making a decision about whose voice is valued and saying to some people that it doesn't matter what they think, because God knows better.

Other people used the 'slippery-slope argument' that once you introduce a law permitting any kind of assisted dying, no matter how limited, it will end up being reinterpreted. The

Abortion Act was very restricted when it was first passed in 1967, but society changed and the law is now being interpreted differently so that abortion is more freely available. The slippery-slope argument goes that once you start allowing assisted suicide for terminally and incurably ill people, then soon you'll be killing mentally incompetent adults and people with a limp. My answer to this is that as society changes and laws become outdated, politicians should have the courage to address the issues and encourage debate to make sure that the law properly represents what is acceptable to society. Maybe all laws should have a twenty-year lifespan, after which they are reassessed. Ultimately, though, the interpretation of a law cannot be changed without Parliament's acquiescence. The crampons are there, they're just not being used, so unless Parliament allowed a slippery slope it would not happen.

When Lord Joffe's next bill was thrown out in 2005 I decided it was time to get involved. I called the Voluntary Euthanasia Society and asked, 'What can I do?'

I had experience of sales and marketing. Surely my skills could be of some use?

Mark, the communications manager, sent me a box of letters to stuff into envelopes, address with pre-printed sticky labels and send. Omar raised his eyebrows when he looked at the heaps of paper that had taken over our dining table but knew better than to say anything. I was a woman on a mission and this was a fight that I needed to win. If it meant folding sheets of paper and sticking stamps on envelopes, it was worth it.

Lots of people entered the debate. Brian Clark's play *Whose Life Is It Anyway?* was revived in London's West End in 2005, with *Sex and the City* actress Kim Cattrall in the lead role, as a sculptress who had been paralysed from the neck down in a car accident and who has spent the last five months propped up in a hospital bed, dependent on carers for every basic function. She has a paralysed body but nothing has affected her independent spirit, sharp mind and biting wit. She makes it clear to the doctors that she doesn't want to continue living like this. 'Nonsense,' they say. 'You're just depressed.' She argues that she has had plenty of time to think it through and she is not suffering from depression but has made a rational decision that she would like to die, please. Instead of helping her to achieve this, the doctors section her under the Mental Health Act.

I went along to see the play with a group of staff and supporters from the Voluntary Euthanasia Society, including Lord Joffe and his wife. It was an old theatre and there was no space for wheelchairs as all their seats were attached to the floor, but they positioned a wooden board over a set of steps that my chair could rest on. I had a great view of the stage, but at one point, when I turned to say something to Omar, my chair shifted and I nearly ended up in Lord Joffe's lap. I'd only just been introduced to him before the play and I was mortified that I nearly got so close so quickly!

The play presents different points of view – including those of the doctors and the heroine's family – and leaves the audience thinking through the issues along with the characters. I thought it was brilliant to see a strong, sassy, sexy woman like Kim Cattrall taking a role like this, but some newspapers criticised her casting, saying that she was far too attractive and that no one would believe someone so beautiful would want to kill themselves.

Of all the arguments I've heard, this one is my all-time favourite. That's it, then. Problem solved. Next time someone wants to go to Dignitas, we can offer them plastic surgery instead!

The play did make me think about the fact that I had changed my mind about my sterilisation. Once Cattrall's character was dead, she wouldn't be able to change her mind. At the moment there are no safeguards – not for me with sterilisation, not for Sue Lawson. I began to see that we need robust safeguards that give people the tools to explore the situation properly before a final decision is made. A prohibition on considering assisted dying also means there is a prohibition on talking about the reasons that path might be chosen. A law change would offer more safeguards against wrong decisions than the current law did, but parliament would have to step up and discuss society's needs.

I needed something to get my teeth into, and it seemed there was plenty of opportunity here to give some dangerous people a sharp nip!

Chapter 18

My High-Tech House

Although I have been using a wheelchair full-time since 2001 and can no longer walk, I don't for a minute accept that I will be in one for ever. My dad's not around to develop a cure for MS, but there are some remarkable scientists doing research into the possible ways to halt its progression and possibly even reverse some of the damage, and you can bet I'm going to be at the front of the queue when any effective treatments are approved.

By 2002, though, it was getting harder and harder to live in my Bradford home. Social services offered me a disabled facilities grant to have alterations made, but I had my own strong opinions about what I wanted and unfortunately they differed from my occupational therapists' views.

'I don't want to live in a hospital!' I protested whenever the subject came up. I thought some of the changes they were proposing were a waste of money and, in typical Debbie fashion, was convinced I knew best, so the upshot was that it was 2005 before anything got done, and meanwhile I went to ridiculous lengths to get myself through the day.

There was a short flight of steps from my front door down to the pavement, so when we were going out anywhere Omar had to lift my wheelchair to the bottom of the steps while I clung to the handrail, then swung my weight round and dropped down on to the chair. As my arms got weaker, that became more and more difficult to do, so Omar had to take my weight and virtually lift me every time. I gave him a thank-you present – a hernia!

I became incapable of hauling myself up to the first floor to sleep at night or to have a shower. If Omar wasn't around to help me I slept on the sofa downstairs and I arranged to have showers at a place called Wagtail Close, which is a group of self-contained flats for young people with disabilities. It was a £6 taxi ride across town, but Carolyn's husband Chris often drove me there. I'd have a shower in their disabled facilities, stop for a cup of coffee and a chat, and then Chris would drive me home again. I knew it was ridiculous to have to drive across town to wash, but I stubbornly held out.

At last the cost of the taxi fares when Chris wasn't available tipped the balance and in 2004 I agreed it was time to go ahead with the house conversion. The council put me in touch with an amazing builder called Terry (they usually just give you a list, but I think they wanted to make sure it was done and done right) to work out how best to rearrange things. He'd made some disabled conversions for family and was so good at it he'd specialised.

The first step was to build a concrete ramp outside the house, so that I could wheel myself up to my own front door.

A simple thing, but it made life so much easier and meant I could get myself out of the house to a taxi without any help.

Terry and I pored over the plans for the interior, along with an architect. Installing a lift to the first floor, either a stair lift or a box going through the floor, would have been simplest, but I didn't want that because it would take up so much space in the middle of the house (and a Bradford terrace can't be described as spacious). If I couldn't get upstairs, the only alternative was to convert the ground floor of the house, and that's the option I preferred.

The sitting room could become a bedroom with an ensuite wet room on the ground floor, they suggested. An extension could be built for a brand-new kitchen, and the remaining bit of garden could be raised up into a little patio area that I could wheel myself out on to. Instead of starting just opposite the front door, the stairs could be curved round so they were accessed from the new living area, which used to be the kitchen. That all sounded fine. Omar could still use the first and second floors to store his things and as a studio in which he could write and practise his music, but I would live on the ground floor from now on.

We started planning what I would need in each of the ground-floor rooms.

'There will be space for a single bed there,' the architect said, pointing at the plans, 'and a cupboard over here.'

Social services would provide a single profiling bed with an electric motor to help me to sit up and raise my legs, but they didn't take responsibility for Omar having somewhere to sleep. I was pretty dumbfounded that anyone would assume I would choose a profiling bed over sleeping with my husband (hadn't they met Omar?). When I said this, everyone was apologetic and they agreed to knock down the chimney breast to fit our bed in.

Social services would give me the cost of the single profiling bed and we could get a double if I made up the difference, but I didn't have the money to do that. Instead we got a bed lever, which I could use to pull myself up, and there was to be an overhead hoist anyway.

I was looking forward to having work surfaces at my own level and cupboards that I could access easily without pulling the contents down on my head, but I wanted something stylish. I had seen a kitchen I really liked at Magnet in Harrogate, and with the help of one of their staff members I picked the units that I could use and presented the plan to Wendy, one of my occupational therapists.

'Aren't you being a bit selfish about this?' Wendy asked.

'What do you mean?'

'It's lovely that you will be able to reach everything, but Omar lives here as well and he's six foot two. Do you want to give him a permanent stoop?'

'Oh.' In my enthusiasm, that hadn't occurred to me, even though Omar cooked our evening meal most nights. Bending down to chop and cook at my level would have been like Gulliver in the land of the Lilliputians. (OK, not quite, but almost.)

'There's a solution,' Wendy explained. 'You can get rise-and-fall units that go up and down at the touch of a button.'

I didn't believe it till I'd actually seen it installed, but my entire kitchen work surface, with built-in hob, can rise and fall by about 2 feet thanks to a hydraulic system. This means that I can make a cup of tea without reaching up to shoulder height to pour boiling water, while Omar can stir the rice without bending double to reach the pot. What genius thought that one up?

Still I argued that while I wanted some parts of the conversion, I didn't want others. If I could manage something by myself, I didn't want any devices or gadgets that would do it for me, because that was taking the pessimistic view. Maybe I wouldn't ever need that kind of help.

'We're only going to do this once,' social services told me. 'We can't plan around what you were able to do last week. We have to think about what's likely to be the case in a year's time, because we're not going to do it again.'

That's what I struggled with – the looking ahead. I never did that. I couldn't. I don't want to think about what life will be like if I can't use my arms, if I can't swallow food any more, or can't talk. I'm just not going to think about it. My hope is that those scientists hurry up with that cure so I never have to.

Terry told me I wouldn't be able to stay in the house while all the conversion work was being done. They needed to rip out walls, switch off the plumbing and electricity, and make lots of noise and dust. He estimated it would take at least six weeks. Omar was flying over to Cuba to see his mother, who was getting elderly and had had a few falls, and was then going on tour with Courtney Pine, so we decided this was the time to do it. I arranged to move into a guest room at a sister unit of Wagtail Close. The Wagtail Close guest room wasn't wheelchair-accessible, but the sister home's was. I had a room with two single beds pushed together so Omar was able to visit me during the odd break in touring.

I popped back when I could to see the work in progress, or to look at proposed features. It was quite exciting, really. Terry was incredibly patient with me and kept making brilliant suggestions that I hadn't considered before. He thought of everything. The skylight in the kitchen roof opens at the touch of a button, all the windows open outwards in a way I can manage, and when there's someone at the front door I can press a remote handheld mechanism to open it.

Once Omar got back, he had a lot of fun with that front door.

'How does it open?' asked a new nurse who had been in to visit me.

'You have to clap,' Omar told her. He clapped loudly and quickly pressed the remote control, making the door open.

'Wow!' she exclaimed. 'I've never come across that before.'

'Why don't you try it yourself?' he suggested.

She clapped.

'Not loud enough. Try again.'

This time, as she clapped, Omar pressed the remote and the door opened. 'You've got it now.'

A week went by before I had the heart to tell her she'd been taken in by a childish prank.

The gadgets they installed in my downstairs en-suite were brilliant. When I first saw the price I was outraged and didn't think they'd be value for money, but believe me they're worth every last penny.

I have an adapted toilet, a waterproof chair that I can wheel under the shower. I then transfer back into my own chair to use the washbasin, which is conveniently set at exactly my level. They wanted to put a hoist into the bathroom to lift me in and out of my chairs, but I like the ceiling and I still don't want it to be institutional. There are grab rails all over the place so it's manageable.

I agreed to have a hoist over the bed, though, so I can get up in the morning when Omar is not there. I don't want to rely on him in that way. He's my husband, not my carer … and he's given himself a hernia from lifting me. I'm not especially heavy, but my lower half is a dead weight and I can't use my muscles to help him. Although Omar is pretty strong, it's too much of a strain on him to manhandle me every day. He has to do it when we stay in a hotel, and that's quite enough.

The first hoist I was given consisted of huge pieces of fabric, cradling the whole body, like the kind of sling you carry a new baby in. It was tricky to get into that and I needed help to use it, which completely defeated my objective. I was quite frightened being up in the air without any real control, so I never used it much. However, another occupational therapist, Jane Fenn, a moving and handling specialist, designed a new kind of hoist with two separate pieces. I just have to wrap one piece about 8 inches wide round my waist and the other

Debbie Purdy

round and between my legs, like a rock-climbing harness, and fasten them with Velcro and a clip. Once it's all in place I press a button and it raises me up and over to the wheelchair. I then turn myself until I can drop down on the seat.

Before, I was unhappy about gadgets and conversions – I thought I would be giving in to MS, not fighting or thinking positively enough. Now I think of it in a smaller way: just like buying a dishwasher, they make my life easier. In the words of General Douglas MacArthur, 'I'm not retreating, just advancing in a different direction.'

When I get up in the morning now, I can get myself out of bed, wheel myself into the bathroom, use the toilet, shower, brush my teeth and run a brush through my hair, then come back to the bedroom to get dressed (although if I'm not going out I might wear something on my top half and drape a blanket over my knees, because it's a real struggle to pull trousers on). When I'm decent I'll wheel myself into the kitchen to make a cup of tea. Alternatively, on a sunny day (I can dream) I can open the French windows at the back of the bedroom and wheel myself out into the back yard. Perfect!

I was so excited when I moved back into the house after the conversion that I just wheeled myself round in circles for ages – through the bedroom, across the terrace (it seems much grander than a back yard now), into the kitchen, through the living room, past the front door and back round to the bedroom again. The freedom was fantastic after all those years spent hauling myself upstairs to bed and going across town to have a shower! Here and now, I would like to nominate Terry, my fabulous builder, for a Lifetime Achievement Award, both for the huge improvements he made in my home and for his immense, undying patience in dealing with me during the process!

I felt reasonably self-sufficient for the first time in ages after moving back into the converted house, but I wasn't really. There are lots of things I can't do any more, even with all the help in the world. I can't reach the higher shelves in the kitchen, so if there's something I want up there I have to wait until someone comes by or until Omar returns home. (He has been known to take advantage of this, putting his Guinness and any foods he doesn't want to share with me on a top shelf, where they sit, taunting me.)

I can't cook, can't iron, can't do much more than rudimentary cleaning (not that I did more when I could), have trouble getting laundry out of the washing machine, and if I drop something vital on the floor and it rolls under a table I have to wait for someone to get that too. Thank goodness I have two phones!

I don't eat during the day, but I'll have an evening meal with Omar if he's at home. From about 2005 onwards I have had carers. Originally, I believed that they would come in at a time suitable to social services and that I would have little or no control. I was wrong. Bradford were trialling a scheme called 'direct payments' whereby social services would assess my needs and, rather than arrange for someone to visit and carry out those tasks, they would pay me the money and I could arrange an appropriate person. There are systems in place to make sure it isn't abused – it is public money after all. But I think giving people back responsibility for their own lives works much better and is probably better value for money.

Karl, Vera's friend from Oslo, had produced an advert, shown in Norwegian cinemas, to explain their similar scheme. In it, a wheelchair user is approaching a high street bank when his tyre goes flat. He whistles for carers to come and help, and when he is mobile again he puts on a stocking mask, pulls out a gun and robs the bank. The image was a bit shocking, but the advert was funny and drove home the point that disability doesn't make you good or bad. You are what you are, but people with disabilities should be able to take responsibility for their choices, whether those choices are acceptable to others or not.

A woman called Iliana has now become my lifesaver. We got to know each other after Omar met her husband, Juan Pedro, at a tapas bar in Leeds. They live near us and can be totally flexible about when they come to help me, so I don't feel as though I've joined the army. On a normal day Iliana will spend between one and two hours with me, helping around the house, doing shopping or maybe accompanying me to an appointment. If I'm away for a few days I just let her know and she doesn't come. But if Omar is away and I need help at 11 at night, I know I can call and either she or her husband will drive round straight away. I don't often do that, but it's wonderful to know they're there.

When the late Princess Diana was interviewed on *Panorama*, she said, 'There were three of us in this marriage, so it was a bit crowded.' Omar and I both feel there are three of us in our marriage, but we thank heavens because the third is Iliana.

Iliana has become a good friend, but she also orders me about sometimes, which I reluctantly admit is good for me. My physio taught her how to exercise my legs by manipulating them, which I find very boring, but Iliana insists. I have no choice but to lie on the bed while she moves my legs around as she's been taught. She's good at keeping my spirits up on days when I'm finding it hard to stay positive.

I wanted to be a nurse when I was very little – long before I decided I was going to be prime minister. I also wanted to be a fireman, a doctor, a pilot and an air hostess, so it wasn't my sole ambition by any means, but my auntie Anne (Dad's sister-in-law) was a nurse and I suppose I liked the idea of making people better. I'd bandage up my teddy bears and stuffed animals, and I had a terrible habit of trying to do this to live animals as well. The local cats and dogs took to their heels when they saw me coming. That ambition didn't last long, though, and when I look at the medical professionals who care for me now I realise I would never have had the patience for the job. My attention span isn't long enough. I'd get distracted before they'd even finished describing their symptoms.

So I've got Iliana, an NHS physio, an NHS occupational therapist, specialist nurses (MS and continence), district nurses, neurologists, urologists, social workers, social services occupational therapists – the list goes on. I've also got Suzanne, my beautician friend, who comes to massage my feet, fix my nails and wax as much of me as I can bear. If I get my hair done at a Bradford hairdresser's called Blues, as I do from time to time, I have to shower at home, get dressed and take a cab down to the salon with my hair still wet so they can cut it. I'm sure I could find someone to cut my hair at home, but I like the trip to the salon; it feels more 'normal'.

I have a buzzer to summon Careline if there's an emergency when I'm at home alone. Most weeks I fall in the shower, and I can get stuck in bed if the hoist is out of reach. The minute I press the button, someone will speak to me through a loud-speaker on the phone. I'll call out to tell them what the prob-lem is and they'll send someone round to help me. There's a key-safe outside so they can let themselves in if necessary. If the buzzer rings but I don't respond, they'll send someone straight away in case I'm unconscious. At first it was odd having strangers traipsing into the house and finding me naked on my bathroom floor, but I've made friends with all the Careline staff now. Thank goodness they're there!

I've always been quite proactive about the care I receive on the NHS and I've been lucky to have health professionals who listen to me and take me seriously. My GP, Wendy Leedham, is a case in point. In 2008 I started putting on weight, which I hate, and while watching an episode of *Casualty* on TV I heard about a syndrome called hyperthyroidism, in which people have overactive thyroid glands and lose weight dramat-ically. Once they start taking medication, their metabolism stabilises. I stopped listening at this point, not interested in the medical facts or that the character had ended up in hospital for a reason. That's exactly what I need, I decided, and wheeled myself down to the surgery.

All credit to her, Dr Leedham didn't roll her eyes and sigh deeply while talking to me as if I were a complete idiot (it must have taken a lot of self-control not to). 'I'm not saying I won't help you, but I'd like you to try a couple of other things first,' she said.

She referred me to a nutritionist, who was incredibly helpful and explained that I was actually eating too little in my efforts to keep my weight down. I had to eat more small healthy snacks throughout the day, stop taking codeine to cause constipation when I was going out, and up my intake of liquids, even if it meant more frequent trips to the loo. She changed the way I ate, and I felt healthier soon after I started on the regime she suggested.

My weight loss wasn't dramatic enough, though, so I went back to Dr Leedham. She was a little surprised but reluctantly agreed to write on my behalf to my neurologist. The neurologist then wrote to an endocrinologist, who threw up his hands in horror! It seems that the side effects of thyroxine are far too serious to contemplate taking it for anything except hyperthyroidism, so I'll have to stick to the nutritional programme for now. But I'm grateful to Dr Leedham for letting me find this out for myself. She knows me well enough to understand that I need to explore options myself in order to realise when I'm being ridiculous.

I've talked to her about the most stupid things over the years and, like an indulgent mother, she never dismisses my concerns. She doesn't agree with physician-assisted dying, but our lines of communication have always been very open and honest. If it were essential to have your GP's consent to die, I'd have to sign on with another GP. In the meantime she's the best doctor I can imagine.

My advice to anyone with a long-term illness is to keep communicating. Tell the doctors what you feel and what you want. Don't be shy! If you don't feel comfortable talking openly to your doctor, talk to a nurse, physio or anyone else who can pass on your concerns to a doctor. If they don't know what you're worried about, they can't even try to address it. Of course, as I know only too well, the patient is not always right (ahem!), but they should be allowed to give opinions about what suits their lifestyle and personal ethos.

The same year social services offered me an electric wheelchair. I just wasn't managing a self-propelling one as my arms got weaker, and the distances I could travel were shrinking all the time. The minute there was the tiniest kerb outside a shop, I couldn't get into it. The electric chair is a lot heavier than my last one, but it is fantastic in every other way. When fully charged, it can carry me about 13 miles without stopping, has a top speed of 4 miles an hour, and it has a kerb-climber so I can get up single steps in it. The charger is tiny, with a 13-amp fuse, so I can plug it in wherever I am, even recharging it on trains using the sockets other people use for their laptops. I'd never run out of charge anywhere – until after I wrote this, when on my way home my battery ran out for the first time and the local Co-op provided a warm environment and a 13-amp socket that a beer fridge was plugged into for me to recharge with.

Once I got used to the electric chair, it gave me a burst of freedom, just as the original wheelchair had when I started using it full-time back in 2001. I hadn't consciously realised how many trips I was avoiding or putting off because I didn't have the energy until I got my new chair and felt confident about going anywhere again.

An added bonus was that for the first time in over ten years Omar and I were able to walk along a street hand in hand. Before that, I either had my hands on the wheels, or he was behind the chair pushing me. It was the one thing he said he had missed, and as soon as we started doing it again I realised how much I had missed it as well. Of all the technical gadgetry I'd been given to help deal with the problems of disability, this was the one that meant the most.

Chapter 19

Some Real-Life,
Grown-Up Decisions

Once Omar started playing regularly with Courtney Pine I was no longer needed to manage his career to the same extent, because Courtney had his own very efficient manager who arranged gigs and transport and publicity. I threw myself into working for Dignity in Dying, as the Voluntary Euthanasia Society was now called, and through this I came to understand more fully the reality of some of the life-and-death decisions people make.

We all know there are 'good' deaths and 'bad' deaths. A good death is relatively painless and comes at the end of a long life, hopefully with family by the bedside able to say their last farewells, a reflection of the life they lived. The worst deaths can mean months and even years of unbelievable torment, when no pain relief works effectively and every moment is a living nightmare. Those who argue that palliative care is always appropriate should meet some of the families of people who endure appalling suffering and beg fruitlessly to be allowed to end their lives. Polly Toynbee wrote a moving article for the *Guardian* about her mother's death, while John Humphrys has written a book, *The Welcome Visitor*, describing his father's final months. There are hundreds more stories like these that are never told. None of this should happen in a civilised society, but bad deaths are common. We probably all know people who will go through what Polly Toynbee calls 'state torture' at the end of their lives.

Modern medicine cannot deal with all forms of pain. Sometimes the pain relief doesn't work, or the patient can't tolerate it. Doctors are pretty good at relieving some pain but not so good with others. Sometimes you have to choose between pain and the side effects of the 'relief'. What one person finds bearable, another might not. I don't think you can either promote or prohibit one course of action, because it depends on the patient.

Some people would rather not stay alive if they feel they've lost an acceptable quality of life. Diane Pretty was, at the end, totally paralysed, unable to swallow, talk or do the things she found pleasurable. There's also the mental anguish of fearing what the end might bring. In Diane's case, her greatest fear was to choke and suffocate, and tragically that is exactly what happened to her. What were her feelings in those final moments of consciousness? Sheer blind terror, I imagine.

The problem is that if you wait until you are paralysed, it is too late to take your life on your own and you will need the assistance of a friend, relative or sympathetic doctor to end your life. When should I kill myself? My hands are losing their dexterity and I'm no longer able to push pills out of a blister pack or undo a childproof bottle, so it would be hard for me to take an overdose now without help. Besides, I'm prone to choking, so I might cough them all back up again. Have I left it too late? Should I have gone sooner? But I still have a full and fascinating life that I have no desire to leave.

Maybe I could wait a little longer if I go to Dignitas, but I would have to be capable of getting myself there, or I would risk whoever took me being arrested and charged with aiding and abetting a suicide. I certainly wouldn't want to leave it so late that someone else had to be involved, in which case they could be charged with murder.

Heather Pratten was prosecuted for helping her son to die. Nigel had the neurological disorder Huntington's disease, which causes all kinds of dreadful physical and psychological symptoms. He had watched his father die a prolonged death from the disease, spending over ten years in hospital, and he didn't want to go through the same thing. On his 42nd birthday he said to his mum, 'The best present you could give me would be to help me to die.'

Heather did her best to make him change his mind, but finally agreed to sit with him while he took a fatal overdose of heroin so that he didn't have to die alone. He was terrified that it wouldn't work and he would survive but in an even worse condition than before, so she cuddled him until he lost consciousness and then she held a pillow over his face. What must that experience have been like for a loving mother? It's unthinkable.

Heather was arrested and charged with aiding and abetting a suicide, and when the case came to court, she pleaded guilty. The judge gave her a conditional discharge for a year because of the 'exceptional circumstances' but warned that others might not be treated so leniently.

How could anyone think that Heather Pratten deserved to be prosecuted? It was an outrageous waste of public money and totally inhumane treatment of a woman who was grieving the loss of her son. With each new story I heard, I was becoming increasingly enraged and frightened about losing control of my life.

In contrast to these horrific cases, in January 2006 I read about the very dignified death of Dr Anne Turner, a retired doctor who had been diagnosed with a neurological disease called progressive supranuclear palsy (PSP). As she explained in the letters she left behind, PSP is near the top of the list of diseases that doctors pray they will never get. The actor Dudley Moore died of it in 2002 and at the end of his life he could no longer walk, talk, swallow or even blink his eyes. Rather than go the same way, Dr Turner decided to commit suicide. She made one attempt to kill herself in her own home, but it was unsuccessful. If a doctor can't guarantee success, what are the odds for the rest of us?

Dr Turner then explained to her family that she would like to go to Dignitas to die, and her three children eventually said they would go with her. On 24 January 2006, in the Zurich clinic, she drank a barbiturate prescription, with her children there holding her hands. However, as she said in letters she left behind, she could have lived a lot longer if she had been able to request an assisted death in Britain. She felt she had been forced to die before she was completely ready to do so, and in a foreign country, simply so that she could do it on her own without implicating her children.

A BBC dramatisation of Dr Turner's story attracted a lot of comment. It was extremely moving television, and Julie Walters, who was playing Anne, gave an incredible BAFTA-winning performance as that bright, intelligent woman.

Because of the terrible experiences people were continuing to have at the end of their lives and because people were having to travel abroad to die, after Lord Joffe's bill was finally defeated, Dignity in Dying decided to support a legal case in order to test the law on end-of-life choices.

At that time I was a board member of Dignity in Dying and wanted desperately to challenge the law. I loved my life but was so scared as my MS progressed. The case they first supported was that of Kelly Taylor, a seriously ill Bristol woman. Kelly suffered from a range of rare and debilitating diseases, including Eisenmenger's syndrome, which meant her heart and lungs didn't work properly, and Klippel-Feil syndrome, which was making the vertebrae in her spine fuse together. Her health had been deteriorating since she was 7 years old and by the age of 30 she was confined to a wheel-chair and needed oxygen supplied through a breathing tube. She was in constant pain because of an allergy to the painkilling drugs that usually treat Eisenmenger's. Her sleep was disturbed by nightmares caused by the medication she was taking. She had bedsores, breathlessness and, she felt, very little quality of life.

In August 2005, at the age of 30, Kelly decided to starve herself to death, because it was the only way she could commit suicide without getting her husband, Richard, into trouble with the law. Even though no one had yet been prosecuted for accompanying a loved one to Dignitas, she didn't want to take the risk, and besides, she wanted to die in her own country, at home with her loved ones. She stopped eating and her hunger strike received a lot of public support, but the agonising pains of starvation became too much for her after nineteen days without food and she had to give in.

Kelly tried to persuade her doctors to increase her medication to a level that would cause her to be deeply sedated, and then to withdraw food and hydration, following the terms of a living will she had written. They refused and that's why she decided to take her battle to court.

'I have had enough of my illness,' she said. 'I have made the decision because enough is enough. I'm just hanging on. I don't want to be here. I don't want to suffer any more.'

Kelly's solicitors argued that they weren't asking doctors to do anything illegal. 'The only way she can be free from pain is if the pain relief doses are increased to the level where she loses consciousness.' They argued that to refuse this was contrary to Article 8 of the European Convention on Human Rights, which bans 'inhuman and degrading treatment'.

However, the British Medical Association came out on the other side, saying that it was 'unlawful and unethical' to give someone morphine with the intention of ending their life. That old double-effect argument again! With the full weight of medical opinion behind them, Kelly's doctors began to put pressure on her to try some non-drug treatments, such as intensive physiotherapy, to help relieve her constant pain. In court, they kept saying to her that she hadn't looked at all the alternatives and that there were different kinds of treatment she could try.

Kelly felt she had already considered the options carefully, but the weight of medical opinion built up and in the end she felt compelled to withdraw her case. She was very upset about it. A victory would have paved the way for people in the UK to ask doctors to use doses of medication that would shorten their lives – basically legalising what we all know happens already in some cases. But it wasn't to be. How desperate does someone have to get? Not eating for nineteen days is a pretty clear, unequivocal sign that a person no longer wants to live, but Kelly felt she was forced to carry on.

Now my case was being considered. 'I know you may die from the symptoms of your MS, but you're not terminally ill,' Deborah Annetts, the chief executive at the time, objected.

'I need to know what's likely to happen if I ever reach the stage where I want to die. I can't relax and truly live unless I know.'

Dr Anne Turner's situation really held sway with me. I didn't want to have to end my life before I was ready just so that I could protect loved ones from an unfair threat of prosecution. But what if I waited and my disease progressed to a stage where I wasn't capable of getting myself to Dignitas? What if Omar had to take me (always assuming he would agree to do so)? So far, in 2007, no one had been prosecuted for taking a relative to the Zurich clinic, but Omar was black, Cuban and English wasn't his first language. He might just be the one they decided to throw the book at. Educated, middle-class white people might be able to find ways to work around the law, but statistically, if you are black, you are more likely to be arrested and found guilty of crimes. I couldn't take the risk that Omar would be imprisoned after my death. I didn't even want to take the risk of him being arrested.

Deborah agreed, but first I needed to stand down from the Dignity in Dying board. We decided to consult a law firm called Bindmans, who were prominent in the fight for human rights. I already knew about Geoffrey Bindman because of his support for a campaign to free five Cubans jailed in Miami, allegedly for spying. In fact they had been monitoring the activities of anti-Cuban terrorist groups who over the decades had been responsible for the deaths of more than 3,500 Cubans, and they had tried to work with the American author-ities, but they were arrested in 1999, charged with spying and given sentences ranging from fifteen years to life. They've been in jail ever since and their families are seldom allowed to visit them because US immigration authorities won't give them visas. So far the massive international campaign to free them has had little effect on the American government.

Geoffrey Bindman can't force American courts to free the Miami Five, but his practice has won some impressive human rights victories over the years, defending people with mental health problems and working with the Commission for Racial Equality and Amnesty International. We made an appointment to go and see a female lawyer in his practice, Saimo Chahal, in early June 2007.

Before that, I had to have a serious conversation with Omar. He knew that I had been seriously upset by Diane Pretty's case and several others that had hit the headlines since then, but he didn't want to think about how they affected me directly. At first he had said, 'It's never going to get that bad.' Then, as the disease progressed, he had said, 'We'll cross that bridge when we come to it.' Now, with the court case, I was going to be forcing him to confront the possibility of my suicide, and his potential involvement in it, which would be a tough call for anyone.

I began, 'Omar, if the quality of my life ever became unbearable ... I don't know what that would mean exactly. I mean, I used to enjoy sports, but I didn't define myself by my love of sports and I have a good life in a wheelchair without being so active. I suppose I define myself by my ability to think and feel and communicate. If I ever lost the ability to articulate what I think, then life might become unbearable for me. Then again, I would rather wait until it happened and decide at that point, because I might be wrong and perhaps there would be compensations. I've been wrong in the past ...' I paused for breath. 'Lots of people have died in my life and not all in the way they would have wanted. And look at Diane Pretty, going in the way she most dreaded. I couldn't bear that to happen to me.'

Omar is used to my long, wandering monologues while I try and figure out exactly what it is I am trying to say, so he listened patiently.

'I know you don't want to discuss this because you don't think it will ever happen and I don't think it will either – at least I hope it won't. But I think it's important to know where I stand, then I'll be able to put it to one side. I need to know to be able to do that. Clarification of the law would mean that I can hang around for as long as I want to, for as long as my quality of life is good. I don't think the day will ever come, I really don't, but if one day it came to it and I said to you that I had had enough and I wanted to go to Dignitas to die, what would you think? Would you come with me? You can think about it for a while if you want.'

He looked so sad that I wanted to take the words back as soon as I had said them.

'Of course I would come, Debbie. I don't even have to think about it. But for now can we not talk about it? Can we just get on with enjoying our lives together?'

I grabbed his face and kissed him passionately, trying to erase the awful sadness in his beautiful brown eyes.

Chapter 20

My Day(s) in Court

Saimo Chahal is impressive. She's a striking Asian woman in her 40s with a no-nonsense manner and a mind like a steel trap. Despite being petite, she has a huge presence and it's easy to see why she's won so many legal accolades and precedent-setting court victories.

At our first meeting I tentatively put forward my suggestion that we could mount an argument based on the Disability Discrimination Act. Surely the Suicide Act discriminated against people who were unable to take their own lives due to their disabilities?

'No, that wouldn't work,' Saimo said straight away, and reeled off an impressive list of reasons that left me open-mouthed and uncharacteristically speechless.

I'd got used to dealing with Latin musicians, whose typical response to everything is, 'Yeah, *mañana*, whatever!' Instead, Saimo was clear and definite: 'No, we can't do that.'

With every statement I made she wouldn't let me off the hook until she had pinned down my exact meaning, because she needed to know she could rely on me.

We went through all the reasons why Diane Pretty's case had ultimately failed, and why Kelly Taylor had been forced to back down, and we agreed that the law was a mass of grey areas. What constituted 'aiding and abetting, counselling and procuring'? If Omar bought me a plane ticket, would he be guilty? If he discussed committing suicide with me, could that implicate him? Committing suicide in itself wasn't an offence. Why was it illegal to help someone to do something that wasn't illegal? It didn't make any sense.

Saimo set about considering the legal arguments and collecting evidence for the case. Our aim was to show that either there was an unwritten policy of not prosecuting friends and relatives who accompanied loved ones to Dignitas to die with dignity, or indeed there was no policy because nobody had taken an overview but nonetheless in practice no one was being prosecuted. Via Dignitas, Saimo prepared and sent a questionnaire to all the friends and relatives who had accompanied a UK resident to the Swiss clinic. The questionnaire also asked questions about people's experience of the whole process and what it involved.

At that time just over ninety British people had ended their lives there, and if even half of them responded, that would give us an interesting picture of how it was working.

Saimo's questionnaire asked all kinds of things to establish what sort of people were going to Dignitas. What illness were they suffering from? What had been their experience of medical help and support in the UK? What was their experience of going to Dignitas? Were they questioned by police on their return, and if so, what was their experience at police hands? How far did the process go? It was the first time anyone had gathered together all this information and it made very interesting but upsetting reading.

Out of the ninety or so families who had been to Dignitas, forty-two responded to the questionnaire. We discovered that the vast majority of those who had gone to end their lives in Switzerland had been suffering from incurable, terminal or chronic conditions, such as motor neurone disease and MS. A few of the companions had been interviewed by the police, but most had never heard anything from the British authorities on their return. How are the police to know if you go to Switzerland with an extra person and come back without them? A death certificate is issued in Zurich, because there are doctors in attendance at Dignitas who take care of all that. The British police only find out if someone informs them. These cases can be investigated long after the assisted suicide has taken place, however, so even if people hadn't heard from the police on their return it didn't mean they wouldn't in the future.

One of the striking things was that the whole experience for friends and relatives, though very sad and painful, was extremely positive in the sense that they could actually be beside a loved one who had chosen to end their life in this way at a moment of his or her own choosing. It was very clear that the person who had chosen to die had made all the major decisions and had driven the decision to go to Switzerland to do so.

It seemed completely random whether respondents to our questionnaire had been contacted by the police or not, and we found out that only eight cases had been referred to the Director of Public Prosecutions, at that time Ken Macdonald. In six of these cases he had decided not to prosecute on the grounds that there was insufficient evidence of a crime. In the other two he had decided that it was not in the public interest to pursue the prosecution.

So the decision about whether to push for a prosecution was being taken by individual police officers and the Crown Prosecution Service. There was no consistency and it was a lottery as to whether a case was investigated or not. So far they had taken a compassionate view. Most decisions had not even reached the Director of Public Prosecutions. My concern was, what if you got someone new in that role who was vehemently opposed to assisted suicide? Would that affect the way the law was interpreted? Could it lead to more prosecutions? It didn't seem right that the law regarding something as fundamental as life and death could be subject to such arbitrary interpretation, particularly when a person could be sentenced to fourteen years in jail if they were found to have assisted a suicide or life imprisonment if they were considered to have committed murder.

Saimo prepared a 'letter-before-claim' to send to the Director of Public Prosecutions setting out the legal arguments and explaining that it was important for Omar and me to know what factors he would take into account when deciding to prosecute in the public interest in this sort of case. She also asked the Director of Public Prosecutions to publish his prosecution policy in cases involving an assisted suicide. It was argued that prosecution policies already existed in other areas, such as rape, race-hate crime, drink-driving cases and others, so why should there not be a policy published in this most sensitive area? This was the prelude to bringing an action for judicial review. Dignity in Dying were really useful throughout in helping to deal with the media enquiries that quickly began to flood in.

On 10 April 2008 judicial review proceedings were issued. The Director of Public Prosecutions was asked to explain exactly when he would prosecute people for offences committed under the Suicide Act 1961. Saimo argued that he was acting unlawfully by not explaining the criteria he applied to such decisions, meaning that people like me didn't know where they stood. She said we could argue that this violated my rights under Article 8, the right to private and family life detailed in the European Convention on Human Rights.

Emails pinged back and forth between Saimo and me as we prepared the case. I wasn't always happy with the way my life sounded in black and white: 'Ms Purdy suffers from primary-progressive multiple sclerosis, for which there is no known cure ... She now needs an electric wheelchair and has lost the ability to carry out many basic tasks. She has problems with swallowing and has choking fits when she drinks. Further deterioration in her condition is inevitable. There will come a time when her continuing existence will no longer be of an acceptable quality. When that happens, she will wish to end her life by having an assisted suicide in Switzerland.'

Talk about putting it bluntly! I skimmed quickly over those paragraphs, trying not to think about them too hard.

Our case was going to be quite different from Diane Pretty's case. She had sought immunity from prosecution for her husband, Brian, if he helped her to die. We were asking the Director of Public Prosecutions, quite reasonably, to explain when he would prosecute and when he wouldn't. We were challenging the murky law not only for me but for hundreds of others who wanted an answer to the question. On another level you could say we were just asking for an explanation of how the law was being applied. How could they possibly refuse?

By the time our case first came to court, on 11 June 2008, almost 800 UK residents had signed up as members of Dignitas. (You have to become a member before you can avail yourself of their services.) If all 800 of these people chose to die in the Zurich clinic, and each was accompanied there by two relatives, that could be 2,400 people who needed to know how decisions on prosecutions were made. Surely they had a right to know their position?

For the hearing in June 2008 I made the journey to London with Omar. There was a temporary setback when we found that the disabled hotel room we had booked wasn't ready for occupation, so we had to sit in the pub across the road for a few hours, but nothing could blight my excitement as I rolled up in front of the impressive Royal Courts of Justice on the Strand, a pale grey building with turrets, spires and carvings as ornate as any cathedral.

A crowd of journalists with microphones and photographers with huge cameras was standing outside and Omar and I looked around to see who they were there for.

Then someone saw me and suddenly all the cameras were photographing us, and people I'd never met were shouting questions at me, such as, 'Why are you here? What are you expecting to happen?' and, 'Do you want to die, Debbie?'

Good grief! Were they really there because of me?

I pinned a smile to my face and managed to compose myself. 'No, not right now, but I might want to some day, so I need the law to be clarified.'

'Will you go to Dignitas? Will your husband take you?'

'Only if we win our case!'

'What do you think about it, Mr Purdy?'

We reached the grand and imposing entrance and it would have been cool if we had been able to sweep straight in to the vast vaulted lobby, but unfortunately they didn't have disabled access at the front. Saimo knew the route in through a side entrance and had arranged assistance from a nice lady from the High Court, who accompanied us to a lift. However, the entrance to the lift was right opposite a flight of stairs and it was a tight squeeze getting my heavy electric chair inside. No one else could get in, so there was a Laurel and Hardy moment as they all dashed round to the main stairs and sprinted up to meet me coming out of the lift at the top.

The architects of historic London buildings definitely didn't have wheelchairs in mind when drawing up their plans. When we reached the court where my case was being heard, the doors opened the wrong way for a wheelchair and there was a bookcase positioned in exactly the wrong place, so it was a bit of a struggle even getting through the doors. This kerfuffle somewhat undermined the grandeur of the place for me, but it probably helped to quell my nerves.

Saimo was there, but solicitors don't speak in the High Court, so two barristers, Paul Bowen and David Pannick QC, were presenting my case. They were both wearing grey wigs and sitting on benches near the front. Saimo sat behind them with Omar, and I parked in the aisle. Three High Court judges, also in wigs, sat at the front, and on the other side of the court was the team representing the Director of Public Prosecutions – my opposition, the guys I was challenging.

I wish I could say I understood everything that was said in court, but I can't. There were lots of numbers thrown around – article this and clause that and Subsection 2,060 or whatever – and the Diane Pretty case was frequently referred to. I didn't have to speak at all. Lawyers for the Director of Public Prosecutions argued that they didn't have any specific policy on assisted suicide and therefore had no legal obligation to publish one.

The Society for the Protection of the Unborn Child (SPUC), an anti-abortion group, made an intervention in our case, saying that any judgments made would have relevance for them and that they were therefore interested parties. So after our arguments had been heard, the SPUC barrister stood up and delivered their point of view, which was basically that all life is sacred and no one has the right to take it away, not even the person living it.

While this was going on, I kept having spasms, my back arching backwards and my body going poker-stiff. I don't spasm so much when I am able to move around, but I was trying to sit still and that set them off. Omar grabbed my hand and squeezed it.

After everyone had been heard, the judges said they would announce their verdict in October and we all left court. David Pannick rushed off to hospital because his wife had given birth to a baby girl that morning and he'd come straight from there to the court. I don't think he had had any sleep. After the TV news that evening, my mobile rang and it was my sister Carolyn wondering why I was in court asking for the right to an assisted suicide and whether there was something she didn't know.

I reassured her that my health was the same as when she'd last seen me, a couple of days earlier, and explained what I was doing. I hadn't thought to tell my family about my court case because I hadn't for one moment considered it would be such a big news story.

My brother, Stephen, rang next and I explained to him as well.

'But it's not going to happen,' he said.

'I hope not,' I told him.

I then had to phone friends to explain that I wasn't taking the case because I wanted to die imminently. They know I'm not a depressive person, and everyone agreed with my right to do as I was doing. Even Tina, who is a Christian, gave me her blessing: 'God doesn't ever want you to suffer,' she said.

Saimo had explained to me that we almost certainly wouldn't win our case at this level, because the High Court is governed by precedents set by cases in the higher courts and by the House of Lords. What we wanted was the right to take the case to the House of Lords, which has to comply with European Court rulings, and it was the European Court that had said to Diane Pretty that Article 8 was probably engaged in her case. It all sounded unbelievably complicated. I couldn't help hoping that we'd win an outright victory. Just before we heard the judgment, a couple of things happened.

First of all, in September 2008, the parents of a 23-year-old man called Dan James accompanied him to Dignitas to die. He wasn't terminally ill, but he had been left paralysed from the chest down after a spinal injury incurred while he was training with his rugby club in March 2007 and a scrum collapsed on him. He had already tried to commit suicide three times without success before his parents reluctantly agreed to help him get to Switzerland and be with him as he took the lethal drugs.

On their return a member of the public reported them to the police, who questioned them, and an inquest was held, following which the case was referred to the Director of Public Prosecutions. The whole incident was seized upon by opponents of change, who had long argued that any assisted suicide law could be used by disabled people as well as the terminally ill. Dan's young age was cited – he was one of the youngest people ever to be allowed to die at Dignitas – and the argument was put forward that he had simply been depressed. He hadn't had enough time since his accident to find that life when paralysed can be fulfilling in lots of different ways, and maybe counselling could have helped him to see that. Now, though, they argued, he would have no chance of reconsidering. There was no going back on the decision he had made.

His parents hadn't wanted publicity, but they were left with no option other than to put over their side of things. 'While not everyone in Dan's situation would find it as unbearable as Dan, what right does any human being have to tell any other that they have to live such a life, filled with terror, discomfort and indignity?' his distressed mother said to journalists.

The newspapers got in touch with me to ask my opinion and I started by expressing my profound sympathy for the family. It's a mother's worst nightmare to have to bury her child, so it should be obvious to all that it was a heartbreaking decision for her and the whole family. To those who criticised Swiss law, saying that Dan wasn't terminally ill and could have had a decent life if he'd given it a chance, I just said that we don't have the right to criticise the family or the Swiss when we don't have a legal framework in this country to give us any guidance. If we had a system that allowed people to talk openly to their doctors about wanting to end their lives we would all be in a position to make free and considered choices.

Maybe a British assisted suicide law could have helped Dan James to live, if it had lots of safeguards built into it, such as interviews with specialist mental health professionals and a cooling-off period after the decision had been made. Perhaps

Dan may have felt able to accept other intervention if he felt understood and listened to. The whole thing was a tragedy but his parents should have had better support.

On the day that the Dan James inquest opened, it was announced that Sky Real Lives was to broadcast a documentary showing a motor neurone disease sufferer called Craig Ewert taking a fatal overdose at Dignitas. There was a loud ruckus about this, but when it was eventually screened it wasn't as sensational as opponents had predicted. They didn't show Craig's body after death. Questions were asked about whether the presence of the cameras had forced him to go through with it. His wife, however, insisted it was what he had wanted for some time, but he had done it earlier than they wanted because of the need to be able to make the international journey. I thought it was a valuable broadcast in terms of helping to lift the taboo surrounding death and raised some important questions for discussion.

Then in October the High Court judgment came through and, despite Saimo's counselling, I was devastated when it went against us – but we did have leave to appeal. Saimo had three months to put together the next round of arguments in time for a February hearing.

Chapter 21

Round Two

The controversy around Craig Ewert's film led to the prime minister, Gordon Brown, being asked about it during Prime Minister's Questions and he reiterated his previously stated opposition to assisted suicide: 'I believe that it's necessary to ensure that there is never a case in this country where a sick or elderly person feels under pressure to agree to an assisted death ... That's why I've always opposed legislation.'

Personally, I'd never support any bill that gave the go-ahead to anyone to cart their Auntie Ethel off to the knacker's yard in order to inherit her house. It didn't seem to occur to Mr Brown that this was precisely why legislation was needed!

All this was in the public arena in the weeks before my case was going before the Court of Appeal. I did some publicity of my own, though, including TV appearances and press interviews with anyone who would talk to me. There was a long interview with David Frost for al-Jazeera. I have always respected him so much. He's no sycophant, just a straight interviewer who let me make some serious points. A producer of his show, David Coulthold, had MS and I was able to set the record straight on air by explaining that it is not a terminal condition. A few months later David wrote an article for the *Observer* in which he said that assisted dying would never be one of his choices, but because the rates of suicide and attempted suicide were so high among people with our condition, he wished me well, because victory would give a measure of control back to patients.

In February 2009 Omar and I made the journey back to London for the appeal. We travelled a day early so that we would be at the court bright-eyed and bushy-tailed. This is England: if you don't like the weather, wait a minute. When we went to bed it was cold but when we woke up London was white and silent. The worst weather for decades. Being a hardy bunch, we all made it to court but one of the judges was unable to get in. There were some photographers outside and I remember being both surprised they were there and grateful it was considered important enough. This time we were in a new part of the court and access was simple. Why hadn't we been in this court before?

Once again Saimo was there and Paul Bowen and David Pannick were presenting the case. It lasted two days, and the arguments went backwards and forwards, particularly with regard to whether my human rights were being breached under Article 8. Surely, as a British citizen, I have a right to understand how the law of my country is going to be implemented. It shouldn't be so confusing or arbitrary that no one really knows where they stand.

By now I was becoming quite accustomed to all the relevant article numbers and subsections and paragraphs. It got very technical and detailed, but Omar and I sat in court throughout and posed for photographs outside at the end of each day.

Once the arguments were through, we had to wait two weeks for the decision, which is a very short time considering how long legal decisions normally take. But it didn't go our way. I was really upset when I heard that the court was unable to find in my favour because they didn't consider that Article 8 was engaged. The judges expressed sympathy for me personally, but said that Article 8 protected personal autonomy while a person was alive but did not confer the right to decide when or how they could die. The European Court of Human Rights had taken a different view in Diane Pretty's case, but this court had to follow earlier House of Lords rulings, rather than the European one. It was exactly as Saimo had explained to me: courts could only go by the rulings of the one above them in the pecking order, so the Court of Appeal was bound by earlier decisions of the House of Lords on Article 8. It was hugely frustrating.

However, once again we asked for and were given leave to appeal – this time to the House of Lords, the highest court in the country. This was very exciting. We would have to wait until June 2009, but who said the wheels of justice turn slowly? I felt incredibly impatient, while at the same time grateful that my case would get to the next stage so quickly (in legal terms at least).

We thought we had good reason for optimism. In December 2008 Ken Macdonald had stepped down as Director of Public Prosecutions and his successor was Keir Starmer, a young, highly respected barrister with a strong human rights background. His career highs had included persuading the House of Lords that evidence obtained by torture should be inadmissible; he'd given free legal advice to the two defendants in the McLibel case, when unemployed Helen Steel and David Morris took on burger giant McDonald's; he had represented death-row prisoners in the US and was responsible for the abolition of mandatory death penalties for drug smuggling in the Caribbean; he stuck up for the rights of asylum seekers in this country, and had all sorts of human rights victories under his belt.

Personally, I felt optimistic about him because of his first name – Keir – after Keir Hardie, founder of the Labour Party. Surely he must have been raised in a family who believed in transparency and democracy? He was only a year older than me. Wouldn't his age alone make him more open-minded than his predecessor? Ken Macdonald's attitude had always been a kind of Big Brother paternalism: 'Don't worry. We'll make the decisions for you and do the right thing.' But that wouldn't do for me – I wanted to know in advance what would happen. Surely, given his background, Keir Starmer would listen to our arguments with an open mind?

Shortly after he took over as Director of Public Prosecutions it seemed like a good omen when he published a full list of reasons why he wasn't going to prosecute anyone for helping Dan James to go to Dignitas. He said that while there was sufficient evidence for a prosecution under the Suicide Act 1961, he didn't think the public interest would be served by one. Dan James had repeatedly said that he wanted to die and he had written a letter in which he made his intentions very clear. It was obvious that his parents had tried to talk him out of it on countless occasions, imploring him and trying every strategy at their disposal. If the case had gone to court, it was unlikely that a custodial sentence would have been imposed.

He was quick to say that he didn't intend the decision in the Dan James case to set a legal precedent, but it was a step in the right direction. Not a giant stride, but a small step.

June 2009 came round and I headed back to London with a reinvigorated smile for the waiting press. The Suicide Act was way out of step with public opinion and it was such a flawed piece of legislation that the Director of Public Prosecutions wasn't using it anyway. Our arguments just made sense to me.

Chapter 22

The Tide Turns

While my head was full of legal arguments, Omar had been quietly getting on with earning a living and establishing himself on the UK jazz scene. He had started teaching at Leeds College of Music back in 2000, after they had accepted a jazz violin student when they didn't actually have a jazz violin teacher. Fortuitously, there was one was living right on the doorstep – Omar. More students signed up in successive years, and Omar began to teach at Trinity College of Music in London as well, working with classical musicians, other string players and anyone who just wanted to learn what the violin is capable of.

I've seen him teaching younger kids and he has a wonderful gift for making children passionate about music. I was with him once when he sat in front of a class of 8- and 9-year-olds and played them snatches from *Peter and the Wolf.* As the melodies changed, he made them guess which animals and insects were being depicted and they were totally enthralled. They didn't take their eyes off him throughout the whole class.

I know he gives his older students a hard time and expects a massive amount from them. He pushes them, because talent is nothing without hard work and discipline, and he wants to instil this in his students so that they can make the most of their gifts. I've heard some of them find him scary, which I think is hilarious, but I guess it works as a teaching tactic.

Omar was still appearing regularly with Raíces Cubanas and, call me biased if you like, but no matter where they were playing, his strong stage presence and extraordinary musical talent had the audience mesmerised. At one gig a woman's mobile phone went off just five minutes into the set. Omar turned to glare at her as she fumbled in her bag to find the offending gadget and switch it off. He then added to her consternation by playing the phone's ringtone on his violin. I've never seen anyone blush right to the roots of their hair like that. Obviously enjoying himself, for the rest of the evening Omar played her ringtone again whenever there was a pause in proceedings. Each time, the entire audience turned to stare at that poor girl. I bet she'll never leave her phone on at a gig again!

He was still working with Courtney Pine, but the one thing I kept nagging him to do that he never seemed to get round to was recording his own album. He had written loads of beautiful pieces of music over the years, but he kept delaying doing anything with them. This was partly because we didn't have the money to pay for the recording ourselves and would need to get a record company or studio involved, and partly because he didn't have the time, with his touring and teaching commitments, and having me in England and his mother in Cuba to worry about.

Gloria had been ill for some time and Omar had been flying out to visit her every couple of months, as a result of which we had racked up huge credit-card debts. Then, in August 2008 she died – that was very hard for him. I couldn't go out to Cuba to be there for him at the funeral, and I think it made him realise how fragile life can be and that you have to get on with it in the here and now.

By the beginning of 2009 my independence was diminishing and I was getting more and more worried that we wouldn't get any definitive answers in our case before I lost the ability to travel to Switzerland by myself. I was getting so desperate that I was seriously beginning to consider going to Dignitas if the House of Lords didn't come through with a positive-sounding judgment when we went there in June. I wasn't ready to die, but I was scared of living without any sense of control.

Omar knew the way I was thinking and was scared that I was going to be disappointed because we'd taken our arguments to court already without any success. He knew how much I had invested emotionally in the outcome, and I think he knew there was a chance that if our appeal to the House of Lords was unsuccessful I would be tipped over the edge. His solution was to get on with recording an album for release that same year, so that at least one good thing would be going on in our lives. He knows me well enough to know that I'd never leave him to deal with a CD launch by himself, let alone miss something I'd been looking forward to for years. Plus, if it was released in 2009, the CD could mark the 50th anniversary of the Cuban Revolution.

So lots of reasons came together, and then Courtney Pine offered his assistance – and his recording facilities – and they were off. There was a rehearsal period and finally, in April 2009, they started recording in Courtney's studio, with Courtney himself as producer. Members of Courtney's band played and other musicians came in to do guest spots. I think Omar was overwhelmed by all the people who were prepared to help him make his CD as good as it could be, as well as by Courtney taking a chance on him.

I'd heard all the songs before, of course, when he was playing them upstairs in his studio, but I had tears in my eyes when I listened to the master tapes he brought home with him. They were just amazing. We chose some photos for the cover, and I was tearful once again when I saw the cover proofs and the dedication Omar had written for me: 'This album is a collaboration, not just with another musician, but with someone special in my life, my wife, Debbie.'

The title was *From There to Here*, referring to the various journeys he has made in his life – emotional, physical and geographical – which have brought him to this point. The release date was set for October 2009, so we had a lot to plan and that helped me to get through the months until my hearing.

When I went to the House of Lords on 2 June 2009 opinion polls were showing that a staggering 85 per cent of the population favoured some kind of change in the law on suicide for people who are terminally ill, with fewer, but a significant majority, thinking it should be changed for those who are chronically and incurably ill. Interestingly, only about 13 per cent felt that disability alone was a reason to ask for help with suicide, which I believe shows that the public have a sophisticated understanding of the arguments and do not encourage a 'free-for-all'. A huge range of factors had come into play, and I'm sure that sympathy for all the people who publicised their own decisions to end their lives helped.

Omar and I made our way to the House of Lords in that wonderful historic building on the Thames, with Big Ben chiming overhead and all the centuries of tradition emanating from every stone. Unlike the Royal Courts of Justice, they have good wheelchair access and we got up to the room where my case would be heard in a decent-sized lift. It wasn't the grand debating chamber that is shown on television – we were in a committee room where legal cases are heard daily – and the five law lords who sat at the front weren't wearing their red and gold robes with ermine trim, but it still felt very formal and distinguished.

Right from the start the law lords were impressive. They were asking detailed, pertinent questions and it was obvious they completely understood where we were coming from. 'Can you be guilty of assisting an act which is not in itself a crime?' they asked. 'If the assistance is offered in one jurisdiction [i.e. England] but the final act takes place in a jurisdiction [i.e. Switzerland] where it isn't a crime, can the assistance offered in the UK be called a crime?' Was the law clear enough to enable a person considering helping a loved one to commit suicide to understand the consequences of their actions, or would they need a crystal ball?

On the other side, Keir Starmer's QC, Dinah Rose, explained that he had created a Special Crimes Division, staffed by a small number of specially trained officers who would look at cases of an exceptionally sensitive nature, and that this would include any decisions to prosecute under the Suicide Act. However, it had already been admitted that only eight cases had actually been referred to the Director of Public Prosecutions. Decisions were being made at a local level without coming to the attention of the Special Crimes Division, and there could be no consistency in the treatment of the majority of the cases. So that didn't really help anyone wondering if they would be prosecuted, did it? And the list of reasons that Keir Starmer had published for not prosecuting in the Dan James case was only specific to that case.

After two days of all the arguments being put forward, we were told they would let us know when their judgment was ready to be handed down.

I hurried out of the building and, with the historic turrets behind me and Omar by my side, told the waiting journalists and TV camera crews that I had faith they would reach the right decision. I wasn't sure if I believed it, but it seemed the right thing to say.

Chapter 23

My Own Little Bit of History

While I was battling in the courts, some enlightened people in parliament were having another go at getting a change in the law, taking over from where Lord Joffe had been forced to back down. In February 2009 Patricia Hewitt, the former Health Secretary, had tried to get a short assisted suicide clause into a bill that was being debated, the Coroners and Justice Bill, but they had run out of parliamentary time. In July, as the bill made its way through the Upper House, Labour peer Lord Falconer suggested an amendment that would have allowed people to help someone with a terminal illness travel to a country where assisted suicide is legal without the threat of prosecution hanging over them. He said there should be safeguards in place, such as interviews with mental health professionals, to ensure that the decision was being made freely without any pressure from anyone else, and that a law would be the best way to ensure this.

There was fevered debate in the House, with those opposed reviving the old argument that it could create a climate in which the terminally ill, disabled and elderly might feel they were expected to end their lives rather than be a burden.

Lord Falconer countered that his suggestion was a very 'narrow and focused' amendment that would help to ensure people acted only with compassion and that no one was forced to do anything they didn't want to do. Besides, it was only intended to cover those who had been medically certified as terminally ill.

Gordon Brown spoke against it in the House of Commons and I got a sense that his views were coloured by his Presbyterian sensibilities, rather than the actual evidence. I don't think it's right to dismiss someone's point of view because they are religious, but I think politicians should be honest about what factors inform their decisions, whether it's socialism, Catholicism or Rastafarianism.

Back in early June, I had been in the BBC offices at Millbank with Jo Cartwright, who manages the media at Dignity in Dying, and by chance I saw David Cameron standing talking to some colleagues. Never one to let an opportunity go by, and after a short deliberation with Jo, I approached him. His severely disabled son, Ivan, had died just five months earlier, so I first of all offered my condolences, then asked his opinion about assisted dying.

He told me that a member of his family had been suffering badly at one time and that the doctors had taken decisions to control the pain, and he understood that sometimes these decisions can result in death. It was all in careful politician-speak, of course. He said that doctors have always made these decisions and to clarify the law might tie their hands and take away their ability to use discretion depending on the individual case.

I said that was fine if you had a nice family doctor who was willing to help, but doctors are much more careful since the Harold Shipman case, even though he was murdering people rather than helping them compassionately. What if your doctor wouldn't help?

I tried to persuade him for as long as I could before an aide swept him away to an interview, but I was unable to bring him round to my point of view. It was a shame, because opponents of Lord Falconer's amendment were using the argument that it might put us on a slippery slope that would one day allow doctors to decide to end the lives of disabled people or others seen as less valuable to society. This is a spurious argument, as all suggested legislation has clearly insisted on safeguards to ensure that only mentally competent adults who make the decision to ask for assistance themselves would have access to this kind of assistance. David Cameron is recognised as being someone who would argue for the rights of disabled people and he would have been a huge asset to our cause, but it would never have been a vote-winner.

The lords debated Lord Falconer's amendment right into the night, but when it came to a vote they rejected it by 194 to 141. Still, I thought, it was much closer than it would have been even a few years earlier. The message was slowly getting through.

A particularly upsetting assisted suicide case was being discussed in the papers around this time. Cari Loder had given hope to thousands of people with the MS treatment she pioneered, which I had first heard of back in 1997. Sadly, the pharmaceutical trials, which had initially looked promising, had proved inconclusive and ultimately the 'cure' she had invented hadn't worked for her. By 2009 her symptoms had progressed to the stage where she knew it wasn't long before she would have to be taken into a care home, and for this intelligent, freedom-loving former university lecturer, being dependent on others would have been intolerable.

Rather than go to Dignitas, she decided to take her life in her own home. She bought a helium-based suicide kit on the internet, had a few conversations with someone at an organisation called Friends at the End and then asked a neighbour to take her beloved dog, Scotia, for a walk while she put the mask over her face and inhaled for the final time. Her suicide note read, 'I do not want to be resuscitated.' After her death, three people were arrested on suspicion of helping her to end her life.

I didn't know Cari Loder, but I really felt for her. How sad that she spent her last moments alone with a rubber mask over her face, instead of cuddling her dog and holding the hands of her loved ones. I hated all the media coverage that talked about her 'losing the battle', and my concern was that it was the all-pervasive attitude that an incurably ill person should 'fight' their disease that had made Cari unable to appreciate the small victories she won every day. A battle against an

incurable illness sets you up for failure, as you cannot ultimately hope to win. I don't presume to know what was going
through Cari's head in her final weeks, but that kind of
language infuriated me. She didn't 'lose' anything. She made
a decision based on what she expected her future to be like. It's
just a terrible shame that it had to happen the way it did.

And of course, because she'd had MS, it forced me to face
up to the fact that this disease could one day reduce my quality of life. Several newspapers reported that Cari was suffering
from 'end-stage MS', but that's not really accurate – MS is not
predictable. There is a scale, called the Kurtzke Expanded
Disability Status Scale (EDSS), which rates the degree of
disability from 0 to 10, with 0 being no symptoms at all and
10 being dead! By this stage I guess I was somewhere between
a 7.5 and an 8. I wasn't bedridden, but I couldn't get far without an electric wheelchair. I could still look after myself and I
could use my arms, although they were losing strength. I knew
that in the next stages, if they didn't hurry up and discover a
cure, I would lose the use of my arms, become confined to
bed and eventually be unable to eat or talk. Cari hadn't let it
get that far because she couldn't bear the thought of being
dependent on others. I wasn't sure how I would cope with it
myself, but so far each symptom had developed gradually, over
a period of years, and I'd found ways to manage each one
before the next came along.

A few weeks later assisted suicide stepped once again into
the limelight when the deaths were announced of the distinguished conductor Sir Edward Downes and his wife, Joan. He

had been conductor emeritus with the BBC Philharmonic Orchestra and associate music director of the Royal Opera House and had been knighted for his services to music. She had been a ballet dancer and had worked as a choreographer and TV producer. At the age of 85 Sir Edward had been almost blind and increasingly deaf and had relied on his wife to be his carer, but when she had been diagnosed with terminal cancer they had taken the decision to travel to Dignitas and end their lives together, with their two children by their sides. They were the most high-profile British clients of Dignitas to date and I hoped that this news would help to show any members of the public who remained to be convinced that for some people the service offered at the clinic was a peaceful, civilised and socially acceptable way to end their lives.

The weeks went by and there was still no word about when the law lords would hand down their judgment in my case. I knew that 30 July was the last day on which the House of Lords would sit in the Houses of Parliament, because government reforms meant it was being replaced in October by a Supreme Court so as to further separate the judges' function from that of Parliament. If I didn't get my judgment before their last day I would have to wait until the end of the year, and who knew how I would be by then? It was a nerve-racking time for me.

And then, just two weeks beforehand, we were told that our judgment would be passed down on the very last day, 30 July. Omar and I travelled back down to London and made our way to the Houses of Parliament. Before we went in, we had a prearranged interview to do with Channel Four, outside in College Green. As they were setting up, one of the technicians came over to me and pointed at Omar.

'Is that Omar Puente?' he asked, and I said yes, it was.

'Wow! I saw him playing with Courtney Pine! He's amazing.'

I was chuffed to bits that despite all the talk of death and destruction, we had a music lover in our midst! Omar certainly wasn't 'Mr Purdy' to that guy!

'He's got an album coming out in October,' I told him, ever the saleswoman.

'Excellent!' he replied, grinning.

As we made our way inside to hear the judgment, I was apprehensive. At previous hearings I'd been convinced we would win and I'd been let down every time. Saimo and David Pannick weren't so positive that we'd win this one: they thought we'd have to go to the European Court, and that if we could get there we would win in the end.

The whole Palace of Westminster has an intimidating atmosphere, very grand and formal.

'Every country should have a House of Lords,' Omar whispered. 'People would never invade.'

The event felt even more historic when we found out that not only was it the last day before the House of Lords closed for business, but that ours was going to be the very last judgment they made, right at the end of the afternoon.

We were accompanied into the courtroom by Lesley Close, who had helped her brother, John, to go to Dignitas, Edward

Turner, who had accompanied his mother, Anne, Liberal Democrat MP Evan Harris, Sarah Wootton, the CEO of Dignity in Dying, and Jo Cartwright. We all sat in a row, fingers firmly crossed, as the law lords came in, sat down and started reading out their judgment.

They began by saying that they had unanimously decided that Article 8 of the European Convention *was* engaged in this case, overturning the earlier rulings. I struggled to understand what it all meant until I heard their final words: 'We unanimously allow this appeal.' I was flooded with such relief that I felt dizzy. According to them, the application of the law as it stands did interfere with my right to respect for private life and should be clarified. Oh God! I couldn't help but think of Diane Pretty and wish she could have had this verdict in her case!

In their ruling the law lords said that notions of quality of life were increasingly important in this era when medical advances can mean that we live longer than ever before. It was an issue that wasn't going to go away. Many people were concerned that they shouldn't have to linger into old age in states of advanced physical and mental decrepitude that left them feeling helpless and inhuman. It's such a sensitive subject, with strongly held opinions on all sides, that it was important for it to be clear when prosecutions would result from assisted suicides, and therefore they ordered the Director of Public Prosecutions to give the clearest possible guidelines about the factors he would take into account when considering whether or not to prosecute.

They didn't agree with every single aspect of our case, but they explained their reasoning clearly on each point. Instead of just saying, 'No, you can't have it!' they said, 'We can't allow this because it would affect the law in such and such a way, and we're governed by x, y and z.'

I thought to myself, I don't mind being told no if someone has a good reason for saying no.

The law lords said that it wasn't part of their function to change the law in order to decriminalise assisted suicide. That was a matter for Parliament. Their function as judges was to try to clarify the existing law, and that is why they were asking the Director of Public Prosecutions to publish his prosecution policy on assisted suicide cases.

I was grinning so hard that my cheeks hurt. We all hugged each other and Omar gripped my hand as we made our way outside, where we posed for photographs and spoke to the waiting media. Fergus Walsh from the BBC was there, and Nina Nannar from ITV, and loads of other journalists whom I'd got to know over the past year. I was happy to see the familiar faces. Many of them had been on the same journey as us, and I liked the way their coverage of the case had changed during the year from depicting an ill person wanting to die to showing a confident, competent wheelchair user who wanted to live. I was so excited I'm not sure that I made much sense, but I hope my exhilaration came across as that (rather than abject stupidity). I felt I'd just opened my eyes and realised that my arm was over the yellow cross.

'I've been given back control over my own life,' I remember saying.

Omar said simply, 'She's got what she wants. Now we can get on with living.'

We'd thought it might take ages before we heard from the Director of Public Prosecutions, Keir Starmer, about the interim guidance, but he soon emailed Saimo to say that he would be issuing interim guidance shortly, followed by a period of consultation. I knew I'd been right to feel positive about his efficiency!

Once I'd done all the interviews and we'd posed for all the photographs the media wanted, we crossed the road and made our way down the Thames Embankment to the restaurant at Millbank. As we crowded in, who should be there but Keir Starmer himself! I recognised him straight away from his pictures in the papers. He's a handsome man of my age with swept-back brown hair and a chiselled face.

He was just leaving, but he came over to shake hands with us.

'Congratulations,' he said to me. 'You made a good case.'

I'm always amused that I get the credit for arguments that Saimo, Paul Bowen and David Pannick have spent many long hours working on and delivering.

'Why don't you join us for a glass of champagne?' I asked, and Saimo raised an eyebrow. Was it appropriate for me to invite him to sit down with us when I'd just won a legal case against him? I was never one to have any truck with social niceties like that.

'I'm afraid I have a meeting to go to,' he said, 'but enjoy your dinner.'

Then he left, and we ordered a bottle of champagne.

Chapter 24

Listening to All Sides

After dinner on the day of the ruling, Omar and I went with Jo to Television Centre to do a *Newsnight* interview. They had to apply my make-up in the canteen because my wheelchair wouldn't fit into the make-up room (but they *had* to do it). The other guest was David Morris, a disability adviser to the Mayor of London and chair of Independent Living Alternatives, who is himself a wheelchair user. He was there to be opposition to me, but actually I found myself agreeing with most of what he said as he talked about the need for the disabled to control their own lives. I've been affected by arguments from people like him over the years I've been campaigning, and I hope they've been affected by mine too. We're all strong-minded individuals who can see common goals, if we let ourselves.

David's arguments were reasonable and reaffirmed that some people who oppose assisted dying have real concerns that need to be addressed. That said, I am yet to hear an argument against assisted dying that can't be addressed. I am grateful for the opportunities I have to be able to debate these issues and answer some of the legitimate concerns that people have.

When we got back to Bradford the next day I was so exhausted I went to bed for forty-eight hours. A journalist arrived at the house for an interview and she had to do it at my bedside because quite frankly I couldn't have moved from my comfy pillows if the house was on fire.

I have been surprised by and hugely thankful for the media interest, which has explained the arguments on both sides to the British public, thus allowing them to develop a sophisticated understanding of the topic. I've become friendly with lots of the journalists I've met and enjoyed discussing the issues with them.

Several journalists have spoken to Omar as well and he just takes it in his stride, the same way he's taken the whole business in his stride from the word go.

Sky came to film us for a couple of days, and at one point they asked Omar the big question: how would he feel if I decided to go to Dignitas? Would he agree with my decision?

I couldn't fault his reply: 'It's not a matter of whether or not I think it's the right decision. She has the right to make a decision that I may disagree with if she wants to, and I will support her no matter what.'

I was touched when I heard him telling a *Guardian* journalist, 'All Debbie wanted was a safety net. It's not as if she wants to go to Switzerland tomorrow. I don't want her to ever go. I want her to live hundreds and hundreds of years [we need to discuss that] and I would have accompanied her whatever happened.'

Omar is an old hand with the media now. We've been interviewed by Fern and Phillip on *This Morning*, and by Jenni Murray on *Woman's Hour*, and on ITV News, and all over the place. Obviously Omar didn't get to say much on these occasions because he was with me and I'm the gobby one, but when he did speak he put himself across with honesty and dignity. He didn't sign up for any of this when he met a party girl in a little black dress in Fabrice's back in January 1995, but he is coping just fine.

Publicity is never all one way, though. Sarah Wootton and I had an interesting interview with Eamonn Holmes in which, at one stage, he asked Sarah, 'What do you say to people who think you are using Debbie?'

Sarah just laughed and said, 'Have you met Debbie? Can I introduce you?'

I'm proud that my portrayal by the media in general hasn't been of a victim but rather of a person who clearly knows her own mind. I have to be looked after by other people to an extent, but I've still got a brain in my skull and a tongue in my head (which I probably use too much). You can disagree with me all you like, but don't ignore me!

The most vocal section of the religious lobby is never going to see eye to eye with me. I can understand the religious argument that life is a gift from God and God alone should be allowed to decide when we die; I just don't agree with it. To paraphrase President Obama's inauguration speech, we are a nation of Christians, Muslims, Jews, Hindus, Buddhists, Sikhs and non-believers, so our law shouldn't be governed by any particular religion or faith. Why should I be bound by the rules of a God who is not my own? Why should someone else's God be able to permit or prohibit my choices? All in all, I don't think we should dismiss religious opinions, but I don't think they have any place in law.

Michael Wenham, who has motor neurone disease, wrote a book called *My Donkey Body* and in one chapter he weighs up the arguments for assisted suicide but decides in the end they amount to a kind of selfishness. I don't agree with him, but I certainly agree with his right to say it. I also had the good fortune to argue alongside Michael Wenham in a TV debate. He is a thoroughly nice man, and we share similar views on many issues, particularly about disability. He remains sceptical that assisted dying will not become a disability issue, but I told him, as I tell other people, assisted dying *is* a disability issue, but only as much as it is a non-disability issue. We will all die, disabled or not, and this is about disabled and non-disabled people being able to choose when their suffering is unbearable, and being able to ask for some help once they have decided they have suffered enough. I appreciated his views on the issue as I believe the wider the debate, the more valuable it becomes.

While we waited for Keir Starmer's guidelines to be published, I read everything I came across on the subject. There was Alison Davis's piece in the *Observer* about how she had attempted suicide because of the constant pain she endured due to her combination of spina bifida, emphysema and osteoporosis. Then, on a visit to India, she got involved in working with street children much worse off than herself and now leads a fulfilling life helping them. She says that if assisted suicide had been available to her before, she would have ended her life but that it would have been a mistake.

I am so glad that Alison eventually found purpose in her life, but rather than being an argument against a change in law, if we had a robust framework in place that would have offered her counselling or medical advice, she would have found her joy in life earlier, without the risk that any of her suicide attempts would have been successful or resulted in more severe permanent side effects. It confirms my belief that we need a proper, open debate about what safeguards we need to put in place to give people alternatives. Disabled people have fought for years not to be ruled by the patronage of doctors and religious leaders, so I don't think we are ready to swap that for the patronage of the Baronesses Finlay and Campbell (both fierce opponents of assisted dying).

Chris Woodhead, the former Ofsted inspector, spoke out in 2009 about his diagnosis of motor neurone disease and, since it was the media topic of the day, he was asked his view on assisted dying. He said he believes the law as it stands is sufficient and that clarity would bring its own problems, but he is speaking from the point of view of an educated, financially independent, middle-class Englishman, who could find a way round the laws to enable him to do what he wanted. In my opinion, the lack of clarity discriminates against people who don't have those benefits.

We were told that Keir Starmer's assisted suicide prosecution policy would be put up on the internet on 23 September and that there would be a consultation period of three months, followed by a further three months before the final thing would be published. I was due to appear on all kinds of TV programmes giving my instant reactions to the recommendations, but just before the 23rd I had been having problems with my catheter and I didn't feel able to go to London. Instead, the media came up to my house in Bradford, where I was primed to start giving interviews half an hour after the recommendations were published.

Davina Hehir, who is in charge of policy at Dignity in Dying, came to help make sure everything ran smoothly. We had one camera crew setting up in the kitchen while I was talking to another one in the bedroom and it was pandemonium. We only had half an hour to read the proposals, so I just picked up on a few main issues, as I hadn't been able to digest every detail.

First of all, Keir Starmer said he would be more inclined to prosecute if the deceased were under the age of 18 or had suffered from a mental health problem or learning difficulty; if they hadn't expressed a clear, settled and informed wish to commit suicide; if they were not suffering from a terminal or severe and incurable illness; and if the person who helped them was not a close friend or family member and stood to benefit from the death – that is to say, if they were paid to help or if they stood to inherit.

Generally, the guidelines were thorough and thoughtful and as much as we had hoped for, but they raised some serious questions. Not everyone has a close friend or family member who would be prepared to assist them. What do people do in that situation? And if you are helped by a spouse or close family member, the chances are that they may inherit something from you. If I die, Omar will inherit the house. Does that mean he is more likely to be prosecuted because he would benefit financially from my death?

How do you prove that the deceased had decided unequivocally to kill themselves and had personally asked for assistance? Should this be done using legally drawn-up living wills or advance decisions? A lot of people who go to Dignitas film themselves saying, 'This is my choice.' Would that be legally binding? Would film footage hold up in a court of law?

If you are a member of an organisation whose sole aim is to help people commit suicide, you are more likely to be prosecuted, and the same is true if you have helped more than one person. Would this affect any of the people who helped Cari Loder?

I believe that there should be a legal framework in place that requires a person considering assisted suicide to talk to doctors and social workers so that the alternatives can be explored, and Keir Starmer's guidelines couldn't do anything to address this.

Overall, I thought he was on the right lines, but there needed to be more clarity about how you could prove that a person wanted to die and what constitutes 'gaining' from their death. There has to be a balance so that the vulnerable are protected from anyone who is acting in bad faith, but those with compassionate motives are still allowed to help their loved ones. I thought that on the whole Keir Starmer struck the balance in the right place, as I had expected. The night before the guidelines were issued I sent him an email:

> My confidence in you as DPP is one reason for me being here to annoy you – but it also reinforces my determination to see real change because my confidence should not depend on the person who holds your office. So even if I continue to complain, I want you to be aware that I know you have listened to all sides in this debate and have made the best guidelines you can for a law that is older than either of us and is avoided by elected politicians because it stirs such strong emotions.

The revised guidelines were published on 25 February 2010. Clearly he had taken notice of the contributions to his public consultation and the new guidelines concentrated more on the motivation of the assistant, rather than the physical situation of the assisted.

Society has changed massively since the Suicide Act became law in 1961. Back then, abortion was illegal, and so was homosexuality. Man hadn't landed on the Moon. Martin Luther King hadn't had his dream. There hadn't been any heart transplants. Barack Obama hadn't been born, and there were many states in the US where his white mother wouldn't have been able to sit down to dinner in a restaurant with his black father. It's a different world now. Medical advances are keeping us alive longer than ever, but not necessarily with an acceptable quality of life. Dying is a fundamental part of being human, and it's time that we revisited a law that informs the way we spend the end of our lives.

I'm not even sure exactly what that law should say. With the arrogance of youth, I used to be convinced I knew all the answers and I was certain about what an assisted dying law should include. The more I've met people with real concerns, though, the more my approach has softened. It's not a black-and-white situation.

I became a member of Dignitas in June 2008, after my case failed in the High Court, and because we are usually broke Omar and I now keep one credit card clear so that I can pay for my own death if I feel it is time. In Oregon, where they have had a death with dignity law for sixteen years, palliative care has improved enormously – it's offered to everyone who requests an assisted death and 97 per cent of those people are enrolled. Of the people who get a prescription that will end their lives, 40 per cent go on to have natural deaths. Every day they wake up and think of a reason to live – having a safety net allows them to do that. My credit card, and Swiss law, is my safety net, but we should have one in the UK.

I may never need to use it. I hope I don't. I still pin my hopes on a cure being found. There were some very exciting results in a 2009 study in Holland in which bone-marrow stem cells were injected into twenty-three people with relapsing-remitting MS. Of them, seventeen improved by at least a point on the Expanded Disability Status Scale, and none of them got any worse. In a separate development an Italian doctor, Dr Paolo Zamboni, treated sixty-five patients by inserting stents to help unblock the restricted blood flow from their brains, which he thought was causing a build-up of iron, and two years after surgery 73 per cent of them were symptom-free.

There's still a long way to go and I'm not going to be following every single development, because I don't want to risk the huge disappointment Cari Loder went through when she pinned her hopes on a cure that didn't work out. I know some people are spending their life savings flying abroad to try every new treatment that's reported, but I won't be following them. Fortunately I have a great medical team and I am confident they'll tell me when there's something that's worth me trying.

If I do reach the stage where I feel I can't go on any more, I hope Omar will be able to take me, because he is the love of my life and I want his to be the last face I see. Other people have offered. Kirsty MacColl's mother, Jean, rang me up and said she would take me if I was worried about Omar being charged. 'They'll never prosecute an elderly English lady,' she said. It was very sweet of her and I appreciated it, but she has grandkids who rely on her, and I'd rather it was my husband.

You never know what life will throw at you. Maybe Omar will die before me. As the great philosopher Woody Allen once said, none of us is going to get out of here alive.

The Director of Public Prosecutions could decide that it would not be in the public interest to prosecute those who assist the terminally ill to commit suicide, while those who assist the incurably and progressively ill would be likely to find themselves in jail. In that situation Omar wouldn't safely be able to take me to Dignitas. I hope that doesn't happen. I couldn't bear to risk him going to jail for me. I really couldn't.

Sir Terry Pratchett gave the 2010 annual Richard Dimbleby Lecture called 'Shaking Hands with Death', which was aired on the BBC. In it, he called for a pre-assisted suicide tribunal, and even volunteered to be the test case. The idea that we would have a group of people to assess the physical condition, mental capacity and any external factors of someone wanting to choose an assisted death is a winner as far as I'm concerned. At the moment cases are looked at retrospectively, which means if there is pressure from family members, or some kind of coercion, it's not found until after the person has died. That's not much use to the person who is dead. There is certainly more than one solution to this problem, and I am delighted that people like Terry Pratchett are getting involved.

The argument was muddied once again by the prosecution of Kay Gilderdale in January 2010. Her 31-year-old daughter, Lynn, had been bedridden with severe ME from the age of 14 and lived a life that she described as 'unimaginably wretched'. Lynn had attempted suicide herself and failed, and she begged her mother to help her. At last Kay agreed and helped to inject her with morphine. The Director of Public Prosecutions decided to charge Kay with attempted murder. I was completely pole-axed. There was no ulterior motive, no inheritance at stake, and Lynn had clearly decided her life had become unbearable. What was the problem?

When it went to court, the judge himself said he couldn't understand why the case was in front of him, and the jury returned a verdict of not guilty to attempted murder, although Kay was given a conditional discharge for assisting a suicide, which she had admitted some time back.

After the House of Lords victory I felt I had been given the gift of extra time. I could wait until I was completely ready to die, if that moment ever came, and forget about it up until then. That was a right that was well worth fighting for. But now I'm not so sure it's enough. Cases like Kay Gilderdale's say to me, 'You can't wait if you become physically incapable of performing the final act yourself.'

If I could write the future, we would clarify the law as it stands, change the law in the next couple of years, and in the meantime someone would find a cure for primary-progressive MS. Fantastic!

I don't want to die. I want to know where I stand, so I don't have to decide now about what may happen in the future. I want to carry on living.

Chapter 25

Lucky Me

I don't know why I got multiple sclerosis. I never smoked, never took hard drugs, and although I've been tipsy in my time, I didn't drink any more alcohol than the next person. I used to be very sporty and sickeningly healthy in every other way apart from the fact that for some reason my immune system started destroying the myelin sheaths surrounding my nervous system.

No one in the rest of the family has ever had MS or anything similar, although research suggests that when one family member has it, others have a significantly higher chance of being diagnosed with it. This could be a case of diagnosis by association: when you hear hooves, you think horses, not zebras. Lots of people who have MS either take a long time to be diagnosed or are never diagnosed, but if they happen to have a sister or uncle who has MS, chances are that's what doctors will consider first. No one has yet discovered a gene for it or proved any genetic link.

Some people think that what we describe as MS isn't just one disease. They reckon there are several different diseases that all happen to cause demyelination problems. So relapsing-remitting MS might not be the same disease as progressive MS or benign MS. There's another disease called amyotrophic lateral sclerosis (ALS) that shows many of the same symptoms.

Scientists have found that MS is much less prevalent in countries near the Equator. If you grow up in a hot country your risk of developing MS is much lower than if you grow up in a cold country. One study examined what happened if you moved from a hot climate to a cold one and vice versa, and found that if you moved while under the age of 15 your risk of getting MS soon became the same as others in the country you have moved to. If you moved after the age of 15 your risk is the same as those in the country where you were born. One theory is that it could be something to do with a lack of vitamin D in childhood, because people living in hot countries have much higher natural levels of vitamin D, thanks to exposure to sunlight. Other scientists think it could be to do with the high-protein diet we eat in cooler, more affluent countries.

Some areas produce clusters of multiple sclerosis, for reasons no one yet understands, but this certainly implies there could be environmental factors at play. Other scientists think that exposure to particular viruses is the key, but as yet they just don't know. It's a mystery.

When I was 7, we moved from South London to a house in Windsor, Berkshire, next door to a farm. While my dad was digging in the back garden he came upon some bones that had obviously been there for a long time. Archaeologists were called in and they were identified as Roman remains. They think it must have been some kind of ancient burial site. Dad was very spooked by this and he became convinced that it was bad luck for the family. Even at my young age I thought this was ridiculous, especially coming from someone who had such a fine scientific brain. Surely he didn't really believe in luck.

In London there was a cat who used to come round to our house because Mum would put out food for him. One day when it was raining she didn't put the food out as usual and that brave little cat climbed up a drainpipe to get into the house through the only window that was open, which was the bathroom window two and a half floors off ground level. My dad was having a bath at the time when a cat's head popped in, and it gave him the fright of his life.

'Any creature who goes to that amount of effort to get in deserves to stay,' Dad ruled, and from then on we adopted the cat officially. We gave him the name Lucky, but in fact I could see that it wasn't luck that had got him a new home – it was his own hard work and courage. (Anyway, some would say he wasn't so lucky in his choice of home, because after he moved in with us we used to dress him up in doll's clothes and wheel him round in a toy pram, which is not a cat's ideal way to pass the time.)

As I grew up I realised that luck is a point of view. It's about whether you see the glass as half full or half empty. Michael J. Fox called his memoir *Lucky Man*, but his luck lies not in having a serious degenerative disease but in having the disposition to learn a lot from it and see beyond the negatives. I should be on commission because I've recommended his book to so many people. Some of them have come back to me and said, 'Oh, yeah, I could cope with Parkinson's disease too if I was a multi-millionaire,' but this misses the point. In fact he may have had more to lose than most *because* he is a multi-millionaire.

I too had to drastically alter my image of myself when I discovered that I had MS. My life was full of friends, travel, sports, music and adventure, and some of these elements would have to go, while others would have to adjust. I see less of my friends because it's hard to visit them and hard for them to visit me, but I have been overwhelmed by the way lots of old friends got back in touch once my name began appearing in the papers because of the court cases. I heard from a girl I used to share a flat with in Scotland back in 1985, another girl I used to work with in Hong Kong in 1988 and several people I'd found jobs for when I worked for the recruitment agency in Leeds. There were emails from America, the Philippines, Europe and all over the UK, and I felt as though I had joined a great new branch of Friends Reunited.

I can't travel much now, certainly not to hot climates. It's complicated getting on and off planes, but I still get trains all over the place, and Omar and I like going to Paris on the Eurostar when we can. There are few sports I can manage – my arms wouldn't be strong enough for the sit-ski waterskiing now – but I still have music and my own brand of adventures.

I realised early on that the way I dealt with multiple sclerosis was going to be crucial. I had to see that there were alternatives to the way I had been living before and that some of them were fantastic. Look at it this way: if you are disabled and need help with something, you can rant and rave and be pissed off about it, but that won't actually help, or you can realise that there are an incredible number of people out there who are ready and willing to help you, and feel lucky that you get to see that side of human nature.

Just recently I was at a Christmas party where Omar was playing. I can't use a knife and fork any more because my fingers don't have the dexterity, so in restaurants I normally order foods I can eat with a spoon, like shepherd's pie, if Omar is not there to cut up my food for me. However, he was playing that particular night and the waitresses brought out Christmas dinner for us all. I stared at the turkey and roast potatoes, wondering how I would manage, and the lady next to me, someone I'd never met before, spotted my problem and volunteered to cut up my meal for me. We started talking and got on like a house on fire and both of us enjoyed ourselves, I think.

There's an old Barbra Streisand song called 'People' that contains the lyric 'People who need people are the luckiest people in the world.' I used to think, That's ridiculous! because in my 20s I was trying my best to be independent and self-sufficient (as many of us do in today's society). Now I realise Barbra's right. It's all true.

When I met Omar I was buzzing around at 300 miles per hour, flitting from one place to the next, and our relationship may never have lasted if MS hadn't forced me to slow down and let myself depend on him. He needed me as well because it's not easy being a Cuban abroad – especially when you don't speak much English – but I don't think he would have accepted my help if I hadn't also needed his. So the timing of our meeting was perfect. Three weeks after the first night we kissed, I was diagnosed with an incurable, progressive disease. To some that might seem like bad luck, but I firmly believe we wouldn't have stayed together if it hadn't been for that. If I were given the choice of wiping out the last fifteen years of my life and not having MS, I wouldn't do it because it would mean I wouldn't have him.

I'm not lucky to be disabled, but I'm incredibly lucky to have my husband. Ours isn't a high-fashion marriage. It's a classic that's never quite in fashion, like a blazer and an A-line skirt. We don't sit gushing sweet-nothings to each other – quite the opposite – but we laugh a lot, and I think that's what's important. He doesn't buy me diamonds, but I'm happy with a single red rose, or the teddy bear he once bought me in a petrol station on the way back from a gig. We don't have much money, but Omar's been playing gigs with great musicians like Nigel Kennedy and Courtney, and we have a lot of fun.

My memory is getting a bit unreliable and I've got no way of knowing whether it's a symptom of MS or the onset of old age, given that I'll reach the advanced age of 47 this year. I've got blurry eyesight, dodgy hearing, can't walk, drop things, am prone to choking, and I get so tired it's as though every last drop of energy has been squeezed out of my body. When the exhaustion is really bad, all I can do is lie in bed and I haven't even the strength to hug Omar when he lies down beside me. Of course, he takes advantage of this because it means he gets to hog the TV remote control and there's nothing I can do. He quips, 'I like my women like I like my tea – weak and white.'

Since the court case he's become more emotional than he used to be. He feels things more deeply. A hurt look flashes across his face as I chat away to journalists about the prospect of my own death. I think if I do ever make the decision to end my life, Omar will feel he has failed. He considers it his job to make my life happy and stop me ever reaching a stage where I don't want to go on. I know that caring for me has held him back in his career. There are lots of opportunities he could have taken but didn't because it would have meant too much time away from me. I've never asked him to do this, but I'm grateful that he has.

He's still cheeky to me, of course. The other day he was talking about the violin I gave him in 1996, the one that he calls 'My Missus'. He said, 'It's a bit battered and doesn't look so good any more, a bit like my missus.' All I can say is at least it still makes beautiful sounds!

At the risk of sounding corny, I love him more all the time. He's turned out to be the perfect person to spend my life with, not just because he deals so well with my MS but also because he's still ready to have adventures with me. He sees what's possible, rather than what's impossible, and that's a wonderful way to be.

My dad, the man who thought anything was possible, once contacted the Royal Air Force and persuaded them to let him take a photograph inside an aircraft flying on a hyperbola that would create weightlessness. He shot a picture of Uncle Tony carrying a glass of lemonade, with all the bubbles and liquid floating upwards. It made the cover of *Time* magazine.

I was thinking about that recently, because I'm planning to do a parachute jump in a wind tunnel soon and achieve my own kind of weightlessness for a few seconds. Unfortunately I can't do a normal jump from a plane any more because my legs could break when I hit the ground, but I'll be able to fly in a wind tunnel at a place called Air Kicks. Omar is going to take me there.

To me, it's an appropriate image of where I am in my life right now. I don't want to die. I want the freedom to enjoy the rest of my life, in whatever way I choose for as long as I choose.

Acknowledgements

While I could take this opportunity to list all of the nurses, doctors, family, friends, neighbours, Dignity in Dying staff, HarperCollins staff and my husband, they all know how important they have been in this journey, so I choose to acknowledge all of those people I have not met who have made this all possible. I would like to thank all of the Dignity in Dying members and supporters who have picked up the phone when the campaign has been on the radio, who have put pen to paper when the issue has been in the newspaper, and written to their MPs time and time again when the issue has been discussed in Parliament. I would also like to thank the people who have come up to me in the street, on the train or in the pub and urged me to keep fighting to change the law, not only for me but for them and their families.

Picture Credits

All photographs have been supplied by the author, with the exception of:

p 6
John Stillwell/Press Association Images

p 7 (top)
Tim Ireland/Press Association Images

p 7 (bottom)
Peter Macdiarmid/Getty Images

p 8 (top)
John Stillwell/Press Association Images

p 8 (bottom)
ASP/Getty Images